THE PRYING HEART OF A
LONELY PRISONER

An Unconventional Approach to Poetry

THE PRYING HEART OF A LONELY PRISONER

An Unconventional Approach to Poetry

By Basim Reid, Sr.

Published by
MIDNIGHT EXPRESS BOOKS

THE PRYING HEART OF A LONELY PRISONER
An Unconventional Approach to Poetry

Copyright © 2014 by Basim Reid, Sr.
ISBN-13: 978-0692272343 (Midnight Express Books)
ISBN-10: 0692272348

Published by
MIDNIGHT EXPRESS BOOKS
POBox 69
Berryville AR 72616
(870) 210-3772
MEBooks1@yahoo.com

THE PRYING HEART OF A LONELY PRISONER

An Unconventional Approach to Poetry

By Basim Reid, Sr.

Contents

It is hardly no accident that Robert Frost coupled poetry and power, for he saw poetry as the means of saving power from itself. When power leads men towards arrogance, poetry reminds him of his limitations. When power narrows the areas of man's concern, poetry reminds him of the richness and diversity of his existence. When power corrupts, poetry cleanses. For it establishes the basic human truth which must serve as the touchstone of our judgment.

-John F. Kennedy (excerpt) at Amherst College-

Dedicated to my sisters

Valarie, Latoya, and Whitley

Introduction

The title in itself is controversial in the sense that... As a prisoner we are looked upon as if to be these vile, violent, and/or criminally insane individuals. Like we do not have a soul or feeling of emotion, when that is not at all the case. In this book I give you my heart, my pain, my disappointments, and both my ups and downs. Here I give you the proof that we are after all still human; that we are still someone's son, daughter, father, mother and so on... So to all my incarcerated brothers and sisters, no matter the race, background, or creed; to those of us who have a hard time expressing themselves, now is your chance to have your voice heard.

It is my belief that there is still *some* good in all of us and for those still struggling to find themselves, please sit down and reanalyze your views and what you want in life. There is always a better way of seeking greatness than by means of crime. Even if my thoughts are only able to reach a handful, we were still heard.

Too many of our brothers and sisters are being left behind for all the wrong reasons. Whereas on battle fields across the world, if a wounded or deceased soldier has fallen everyone in his or her unit, even the unscathed men and women will risk their own lives to bring that fallen individual back home. As is our imprisoned brothers and sisters, we have slipped and fallen into an inferior state by way of fighting a war within ourselves, and often times without you we are lost.

So please, if you know of anyone in prison, send a note card, a picture, or even a mere few lines every now and again just to let them know they are not forgotten, and that just like in the "No man left behind" clause, you will be there until they are brought back home. They say that change starts within self, why don't you be the driving force in awakening the masses to this reality. Just something I thought you should ponder on. Enjoy your read.

With Love,

B. Reid, Sr., Author

Foreward

This author Basim Reid has found a unique way to capture the internal experience of incarceration. Not internal in the aspect of behind the penitentiary walls but inside the walls that hold much more relevance, the walls of the heart and soul. Through this assortment of poems and essays he succeeds in explaining the thought process of the inmate serving time. Given, this is only a mere microcosm of the total experience. However what you will see is the common ground that I believe all of us who do time can agree on, and through this uniformity the reader should be able to imagine four walls surrounding himself, closed in like a 8 by 10 cell. These four walls are stress, despair, loneliness, and the strongest one hope. "The Prying Heart of A Lonely Prisoner," is not just a fancy name of a well written literary masterpiece, but rather what Basim Reid has managed to materialize into something that can be held in your palms to read despite the gross magnitude of the emotion and strain. Take time to think about what caused such thoughts to collect in the writers head, I know I will.

Bilal Muslim, Entrepreneur

Founder of Blakk, Inc.

Acknowledgments

First and foremost, I would like to thank Allah (God-S.W.T.) for allowing this opportunity to be possible.

To my maternal grandmother Deborah H., I would like to give special thanks for always believing in me and for sticking by me throughout *ALL* of my trials and tribulations. Lord only knows that without you I would be stuck up a creek without a paddle. Thank you for loving me unconditionally.

Mother, I can never thank you enough for giving me life. You have always been my foundation and I am grateful for the tough love you have given me as a single parent. For, it made me the man I am today.

To my two beautiful sons, Ja'marion and Basim, I would like to thank each of you for being a father's inspiration. Verily, the mere thought of you gives me hope anew and I promise that this is only the beginning of our empire. The best surely has yet to come.

I would also like to thank Verna B. (Mom-V.) for being my guiding light and that motherly voice when I needed to find myself. I can never forget the love and support you and your family have given me over the years. Thank you.

To those of whom I may not have been able to mention, thank you for simply being you. After all, it was our encounters or lack thereof that has inspired the views I currently scribe about in some form or another.

And last but not least, to my cousin Naim Robinson, you have always been a brother to me even before Islam. Thank you for the psychological support and for doing my time with me. Insha-allah, Allah (S.W.T.) bless you both in this life and the next, Ameen.

I

Droplets of a Bleeding Heart

Never make someone a priority
when you are only an option for them

-Colin Powell-

Dear Viana

Date: January 30, 2008

Dedicated to Viana B.

I miss you so much. Sometimes I feel like the words to utilize in describing how I feel about you haven't even been revealed yet.

And then when I do feel as though I've found them, they somehow disappear again into the unknown, making me feel as if I'm losing my mind for even thinking that I could imagine such words, to compare to someone as beautiful and unique as you.

But then I find myself narrowing them back down to one indescribable term...

YOU.

Commentary

This poem initially began as a letter to a very special friend of mine. This woman has challenged me in every sense of the word, so in contrast to exhausting any other formal introduction, I wanted to open such a letter in a way I have not tried before... Writing what I truly felt versus conning her love by means of using calculated measures, in spite of my current situation.

After all, the tarnishment of our relationship was at the hands of my own misdeeds from the outset; when I was a lot younger, for reasons I won't bring to detail. But in the end, know that she and I both suffered from wounded hearts.

In this instant matter, for many of us resentment prevails soon thereafter. And often things become too far torn to make amends. It is not that we do not come to wish that things had unraveled differently, but we are who we are, and just as it is impossible to turn back time or undo what has become of our past, we must understand that we cannot go forward until we say good-bye to what is behind us.

However, truly my love for this woman is more profound than simply stated. Like the late Malcolm X. (Shabazz), I too, believe in the power of words and their ability to influence and engage people, but I am only human. So in finding the right ones to use can sometimes be as complex as the feeling itself.

As a result, what better way to say you do not know the words to express how you feel than stating just that. I would never tolerate or even advocate mediocrity for that matter but sometimes you just have keep it simple, as in its former and present title. At its length I came up with Brief(ly) and Untitled with the intention of later animating a more fitting name. But it kind of stuck and for some time—as it both insinuates simplicity and the complexity of the brewing emotions within us.

Refreshingly enough though, I recently decided to change its title to "Dear Viana" as it serves to emphasize the intended purpose to begin with. A message to the one who got away, which in its own right is a factor a number of us imprisoned and non-incarcerated persons can relate to.

The Prying Heart of a Lonely Prisoner

Longing for Your Touch

Date: May 10, 2011

Since our departure, the days are longer and the nights just don't quite seem to end quick enough... As I long for your touch.

Since our departure, I can't seem to get anything right or find a means to take interest in the things I once enjoyed... As I long for your touch.

Since our departure, while adjusting to your abrupt absence, I find myself constantly measuring the influences another person has over my daily activities in comparison to how your presence once weighed on them... As I long for your touch.

And since our departure, I can honestly say that no one has ever effected the contents of my heart the way you have, and because of that I can hardly wait until we are united once again... As I long for your touch.

Commentary

Written with another good friend of mine in mind, with whom I had met on a pen-pal site while incarcerated. From the beginning things between she and I had gotten off to a wonderful start, yet and still, I maintained my distance emotionally after having experienced a pattern of heartache whenever involved in relationships while in prison. Needless to say, her persistence slowly chipped away at the hardened facade I had put up as she and I shared one of the more successful relationships in the time that I was a member of the site.

Then one day her sweetly scented letters just stopped coming. And that one day eventually turned to weeks—the weeks blended into months—and those months soon came to near a year that I had not heard from her. I had her telephone number so in the first month of her absence, I tried calling and additionally sent several poems professing my need of her before facing reality...she was gone.

I did not know if it is something I had said or done but decided to chalk it up as a loss.

However, occasional thoughts of her still crossed my mind, so in the beginning stages of this book, I thought to put that energy in the form of poetry as well. Since then, she and I have reconnected and now maintain a healthy relationship. She even reviews a lot of my writings and gives her personal opinion on them.

But it does not always end that way. A lot of my prisoner brothers and sisters never get that second chance or in most cases, a first for that matter. We were of the fortunate few. It would seem that once you are imprisoned you are no longer considered alive by those you love. You may cross their mind at some point or another, but in terms of past tense and very few ever do anything about missing you. Because of this a lot of us feel betrayed and left for dead.

I do agree with things being done out of the kindness of your heart. Where I beg to differ though, is indeed a lot of us were the black sheep of the family but nonetheless looked out for the family. Even if it was just keeping your boyfriend from beating on you, being there to lend a listening ear when you needed to be heard, helping out with the bills, groceries, or even your children to name just a few examples.

Yeah, we know how easy it is to forget the little things when busying yourself with life's errands. So this poem is your little reminder. It should be nothing for you to purchase a post or stationary card to let us know we are not forgotten every now and again. You do not have to alter your lifestyle to do so.

The Prying Heart of a Lonely Prisoner

A Disturbed Utopia

Date: July 10, 2011

Dedicated to Shante' H.

My Dearest Love,

From the time I lay to sleep til[1] the moment I awake... I see you. Not so much in the physical form but more so in relation to the figment of my imagination.

Enclaved by what appears to be a glimpse of what I've longed for over the years, yet and still, restrained by two worlds unwilling to assimilate and unfold in unison.

Ever so intrigued by the sub-conscious images of you, where each sighting unravels in its own mystical way. Some dreams are more pleasant than others, but to even be able to envision you at all keeps me in a state of unsettled suspense.

Alas, torn in between the lesser evils of pain and pleasure entirely. For the mere thought of you alone remains to be exhilarating, whilst the story line surrounding other apparitions of you renders me defenseless, devastated, and/or riled up.

Though challenged with struggling to wake on a day to day basis, I desperately long for insomnia and in contrast, during my times of finding difficulty to sleep I resent having chosen a fantasy life over reality.

Leaving my warped mind to ponder one dreadful question... Could you simply be that of my dream girl or just another repetitious person in a slew of ambiguous nightmares, stemming from the taunting of my own rampant mind?!

Commentary

Like most imprisoned men and women, my outside relationships have always been an emotional roller coaster. One minute I am absolutely in love with those involved in my life. The next, not so much. In fact, one of the most painful memories I have is of a 'Dear John' letter written to me by this woman back in February of 2006.

For those of you who do not know, a 'Dear John' letter describes the writer's intent to no longer want anything else to do with you. Unfortunately, for me this letter arrived just a month and few weeks after she had given birth to my son and just ten (10) months into my legal abduction. I was unaware of any problems between us and still

14

very much in love at this point, so it all took me aback.

Of course we reconciled some time later but not too long after, I waltzed on a tier where she happened to be exchanging love notes with another inmate from my town. I felt both humiliated and betrayed all at once having to be housed on the unit with this guy, because I had otherwise always been so proud of this woman. What I did not get though, is why one would leave their alleged spouse in prison for another living the same lifestyle. It's like, if you are going to leave; leave for someone better than me, not someone who will eventually put you in the same situation or worst. That defeats the purpose, or rather, provides not justifiable means to an end. But again, we made amends.

The next heart aching memory was her allegedly having an affair with a last page relative of mine while in their guardianship. Then me having to file for visitation rights of my son, to which I was granted but were never given relief of such on her behalf, and the hurtful deeds and words go on.

Apparently I care very deeply for this woman to tolerate such mental abuse, as she is the mother of my child. But time has consumed our relationship and has since caused many disputes within the duration of my sentence thus far.

There have been times when I have waken up out of my sleep so angry that I have wanted to punch the wall. I have awaken from bad dreams involving this woman, not wanting to go back to sleep because I resented having to see her again hurt me in them.

Every now and again she will reappear whenever she has a fall out of some sort with her then beau and proclaim how "Wifey's Back," again. But only until she finds someone else to take an interest in her and Lord only knows that if I had just a nickel for every time I heard that statement, I would have been able to make bail. That is beside the intended purpose though.

The message I want(ed) to convey to individuals of an incarcerated spouse is: We understand that you have a life to live aside from tending other responsibilities and we respect that. For you are a wo(man) first, but there are ways to do things tastefully or in good faith should I say.

However, prison is the other side of life that the rappers or others don't talk about. Or if they do happen to mention it, they speak of it in terms of being something of a minute nature. They don't tell you how to conduct yourself as a lonely woman, a financially strapped or drug-addicted single mother.

Instead, you only hear of the flamboyant lifestyles of hustlers and con men being glorified. So before you claim not to have signed up for this part when involving yourself with us, you indeed surely have.

When you decided to bare our children, to spend our money and relish in the attention of living lavishly. It was a package deal like the acceptance of a woman who bore children before you, or even a clause in the contract you overlooked in the fine print.

With that, all we ask for in return is that you at least take the two (2) or maybe three (3) minutes out to respond to our letters, or at the bare minimum send a post card to let us know we are not forgotten. Do not turn your backs just because we are down on our luck. Unless this man or woman has hurt you, there should be no reason why s/he should not hear from you. Do not wait until the last hour to reach out, because only then will it be too late to declare your sob story. It is the same as a woman being fed up.

As this poem was written with the intention of revealing the relation of a dream world and reality; enclaved by definition means: A country or a portion of a country surrounded by foreign territory. In this sense, my mind is the country and the thought of her is the foreign territory in that she abandoned me.

The wanting of her represents the good times we shared together, and the more troubling areas of the poem represent the bad and so on. It is okay to leave if that is what you choose to do. But do not lead us on in the process and/or push everyone else away in our corner only for you to do the same in the long run, as well.

Oppressed Romance

Date: October 4, 2011

To be so cruel as emotional abuse, yet what our love entails is as addictive as one's own blissful desires. Your callous words can sometimes be so sharp as to cut like a knife, though so endearing on other occasions.

Your malicious stares, infectious center, and caustic criticisms blended together can erode even the sanest mind, body, and soul just as that of a cancerous disease. Your sex burns at the same temperatures of a napalm fire, but when utilized as a calculated measure to control is just as lethal as mental manipulation.

Spiritual transgression, to say the least, doesn't necessarily leave scars in the visual form. But surely its ramifications are just as real and detrimental as the contact itself.

To be so powerful as to maim without touch... To be so ambiguous and strategically put to together as to insinuate without direct indication... Or to be that of an unintended name hurled in the midst of anger. Building you up only to be brought back down. Empowering yet destructive, rapidly creating a weakness of everlasting repair.

We are all prone to become a victim of emotional abuse to some extent, but lack the insight to address the same accordingly. To feel alone or abandoned by those closest to us are among the most common cases as it pertains to an unhealthy state of mind.

And I know you may disagree but after all, what is a good conscience if it is unawakened?!...

Commentary

I wrote this poem as a close cut summary to an article in an October/2011 issue of Ebony Magazine written by Joyce Morley, Ed. aka Dr, Joyce.

The subject is very sentimental to me because I, myself, am a victim of emotional abuse. I just had difficulty expressing that because I lacked the necessary tools to identify such an act, that is until I read her article. It had been so well written that I could not fathom it being scribed any better. And as a compliment decided to add it to my book but from a prisoner's perspective.

Inasmuch, I remember being so scarred from that first 'Dear John' letter that to this very day I sometimes second guess whether or not to open her letters whenever they do arrive. I have grown to dread the idea of receiving any more bad co-relational news.

But as a prisoner communication is our *ONLY* link to society or the outside world in lay-man's terms. And often that bridge deteriorates to a non-functioning point by way of carelessness on either end.

It has become common for us as a people to disparage on each other's feelings and beliefs. It is as if we as men no longer respect our women and likewise. Here you have it, we will deal with strangers in these streets or any other arena with the utmost courtesy, and turn around to treat and take the ones we allegedly hold dear with blatant disrespect. We have lost our family structure and have begun to alienate ourselves in these isolated groups.

We act and speak as if we hate each other—our own people, including my own once unawakened self. We break the spirit of one another with no remorse and carry on like nothing else matters but the condition of our selves. Whereas we sometimes fail to realize to which the magnitude of the effect and influence of our decisions on others.

Throughout my incarceration thus far, I have been spoken down on by people who would not otherwise speak to me in such a manner had I been released. I have been hung-up on, had telephone numbers changed, or my phone calls not answered at all, even after I have been asked to call. I have been told I do not love you any more, I heard my son call someone else dad; not simply because that person had cared for him, but because he did not know that I was his actual father.

I have been through waiting for visits that never materialized and having to accept the excuses even though I knew they were lies. I have dealt with hearing other men in the background, had associates deal with my then lady behind my back, and have even heard hurried panting on the line of a call as if to insinuate sexual relations, before a sudden disconnection.

I am not claiming to be the only recipient of the aforementioned deeds, nor will I wallow in pity because of them, as there is always someone here who has been subject to an even worst predicament. All these things among others though, trigger unhealthy thoughts related to emotional abuse. It is paralyzing and makes you question yourself like you are incompetent or unable to fend for yourself.

I will not say that these actions are not warranted in some cases, but no one deserves to be treated as such. An act of cowardice, to kick someone while they are already down. It is no wonder why ex-prisoners come home so bitter or angered if you will; not to be mistakened for justification of any demeaning or albeit violent behavior in return.

However, one thing I have learned from all of this is that you as a prisoner have a choice to either allow harsh conditions to make you bitter or better, I chose the latter of the two in spite of (some of) my counter parts because I felt for it to be an inevitable event in my life. I decided to use that hurt as the fuel to change my circumstances and you can too, but it first starts with self awakening.

The Prying Heart of a Lonely Prisoner

Love on the Edge

Date: November 13, 2011

When discouraging factors compels you to reconsider the footing, surrounding the foundation of every relationship you once held dear. Not on account of the intentions of which they were built, but as a result of lacking to fulfill co-relational duties.

To be unable to peer at those very individuals and possess the same ability to identify the similarities that initially brought you together. When the years spent polishing the bonds thereof seem meaningless... You grow to despise the reality you shared and inevitably come to a point where you haven't anymore to give.

As jarring as it is a realization, when at a moment's notice you would have and did sacrifice blood, sweat, and tears or would have given your own life to preserve theirs in exchange.

By far, an oath you held to be sacred; not honored behind imprisonment, when it was said to supersede death. A verbal agreement that never came into manifestation as my 'Free Life' came to a startling stand still. And instead my alleged comrades and relatives alike equally left me for dead in forlorn and engaged the woman I loved in coitus amatory.

A tarnished love via irreconcilable differences, though the saying is to forgive and not forget. But to try and try to reconstruct a building on unlevel ground—a useless waste.

Commentary

In dealing with people, I have learned that you cannot expect anyone else to be you or anything other than themselves. That is to say that few may possess similar traits as your own but no two people are created identical.

While serving my sentence I discovered a speech by Colin Powell that reads in part, "Through prosperity your friends know you but through adversity you know your friends." This holds very much true in many respects and includes but is not limited to fellowship, but also those of whom we dealt with or love(d) on any level.

Before then, the loyalty I gave was no doubt thought to automatically be reciprocated. To my surprise, reality struck and struck quickly. In that event, I found solace in protecting my heart through trial and error. And almost instantly I learned to distinguish family from that of a relative, friend from foe, and the difference between love and infatuation.

So prison has been especially hard on me because as a prisoner not only do I refuse to conform and/or accept defeat, even in my weakest state I will not allow myself to be a victim of circumstance. As such, you become inferior by your own consent. They say that character represents what you stand for and reputation by which you fall. By this truth, I chose to adapt said philosophy by disassociating myself With those of whom have proved to be not for me.

If I had had it any other way I would have inaudibly accepted an invite to playing someone else's "game." That is just being brutally honest. With that, regardless of the service I receive in life, I readily express gratitude by absorbing its lesson and exhibiting growth.

This literary piece clearly speaks for itself and in no way was written to oust anyone in particular, but for therapeutic purposes. The backlash of these acts has caused under my eyes to grow darker from being depressed. I was emotionally devastated as well as exhausted and incidentally met such pain and misery with resignation.

Nonetheless, all these things happening to me was indeed the starting point of an internal revolution. It just so happens that this revolution was recorded by a number two (2) pencil, scribed on loose-leaf and made for the public to see at will. Love on the edge explains just that though. It is too far gone to be pushed any further.

The Prying Heart of a Lonely Prisoner

II

Optimism in Turmoil's Wake

The Prying Heart of a Lonely Prisoner

Women of Wonder

Date: November 15, 2011

Exceedingly beautiful in every shape shade and stature. From the luxurious flow of your hair in varying grades, to the sensual batting of your eye lashes, and the tenderness of your alluring lips.

An immaculate organic structure, contrary to the self-critical notion of imperfection, as you are the only Homosapien able to conceive and reproduce. Surely humanity as we know it would cease to exist trailing your inability to pro-create.

A majestic specimen you are, an impeccable balance of strength and incendiary sexual divinity. For even in naiveté, with every gesture you move so rhythmically and artistically as you fiercely saunter across life's runway.

Everything about you; so intricate and mysterious, that both your physiological and psychological make-up remains controversial to this very day. You excel in sustaining life, protecting emotionally, and providing a safe haven in angst of peril.

Complimentary to the many fallacies of man, as you furnish a nourishing environment derived from an extraordinary dividend of love, warmth and security. Further circumventing poise to logic with feeling.

As mighty as Mother Nature herself, in fact, how her name came to be following the dawn of man. Life's greatest asset and treasure. You continue to captivate and be the great enigma, so unpredictable, so vulnerable, so wonderful and unique to name just a few of your qualities.

For, the many changes your body forgoes all attributes to your abstract beauty. An inner dwelling of a storm torqued by emotion, spirituality, and rogue thoughts as you process all that surrounds you.

Yet to MOST you remain under-appreciated and taken for intrinsic granted, perhaps only until the commanding roles are somehow reversed, mandating a whole-new commendation of the female gender.

Commentary

There are no group of words to be used in effectively describing the significance and wonder of women. In this opinionated conviction, "Women of Wonder" was written in contribution of combating the war-on-women. I have sat by far too long and watched the many and various crimes committed against women and children on HLN, CNN, and other news shows in silence and complete disgust. It is revolting how we could treat a precious gem with such disregard.

The same goes for women who are not accountable for their own actions, as well as it is for us as men needed to step up and be better husbands and fathers to our children. Neither the female-human nor the male-human are asexual creatures, as we were created to accommodate one another. Without the other, life ceases to progress as an individual person is not meant to last forever. Rather, our only chance at surviving in immortality is through procreation.

We were crafted to work together in unity and to help one another capture a more balanced image of life. Yet in grasping the dream of being a dominant people, we seek to conquer by dividing and destroying which ever obstacle that may or may not lay in our paths.

True it is in our nature to be imperfect. But by no means is this to be utilized as a ploy to justify our indiscretions toward women. For, one should never be ashamed to own that s/he has been in the wrong, which is but saying in other words that s/he is wiser today than she or he was yesterday. Instead we should strive to heal and empower the whole of our women to be the queens and princesses that they are.

Presumably we can achieve this by setting better examples to be followed and becoming better role models as men and fellow women. Even those of us who are incarcerated, we can reverse and control this dynamic by encouraging our younger brothers and sisters to reach their full potential; to read more, to associate themselves with leaders as often as possible, and to share the same insight with those we love on the outside of prison alike.

Most times, the ones who do know better, hinder the growth of our youth by with-holding this knowledge of cultural awareness. It could be a result of our opposition of opinion, in age difference, our inability to relate in communication, or out of spite too.

Whichever the origin of this defiled and fleshy mind frame, there is a saying that, "Thousands of candles can be lit from a single candle, and the life will not be shortened nor will it perish in vain."

I remember a time when that was the case. When our elders would reach out and build with the younger generations to be more self-reliant and mindful of the long term ramifications of our deeds. Now it is as if those days are long gone unless it involves some sort of sleazy scheme which reaps a benefit for the teacher. That is for those who do know better, anyway. Then you have those of us who are just as oblivious as most youth, to the power we could possess as a people if only we would come together. I am not saying that we are a damned people or that all of our older life Instructors are gone as 'EXPERIENCE' is sometimes (y)our greatest mentor. But I do believe that we are in dire need of more practical and moral-some educators to make a difference.

34

Not losing sight of the objective; a single female can birth an entire nation, teach their daughters to do the same and so on. And until we see her as such, we will continue to be at a loss with gender clashing. So do commend and cherish your woman as she is like no other.

The Prying Heart of a Lonely Prisoner

Tears Cried Alone

Date: November 8, 2011

A feeling so intense that it can only be expressed via emotion. To know of an unattainable love merely through distance, or perhaps the restricted results of an inadvertent incarceration.

To be unable to awake with you beside me in bed. To be so sure of your own self worth, the qualities you bring fourth and to yearn for that same compatibility, companionship, and affection in spite of it's unknown origin.

To know in your sub-conscious mind, that out there—somewhere in the universe, amongst the stars and black of night, that someone exist for you, but to be unaware of her whereabouts. That someone to share in your dreams, your hopes, ambitions, and most of all your life.

Some would say that it is the by-product of being a hopeless romantic. While others would applaud the ability to remain hopeful in the face of adversity. As not having a shoulder to lean on can bring even the strongest man to his knees.

That is to say, tears shared are not as bitter as that of those cried alone. So optimistically, I know that the foundation of my loneliness isn't of an emanate tear of pain, but that of foreseeable love.

Commentary

I wrote this poem for all the days the corrections officers passed my cell without even hesitating to stop at my door to hand out mail.

I wrote this poem for all the weekends that went by and my name was never called for visit, for the embarrassment I felt after having gone to ask the corrections officer if it was my name s/he called when indeed s/he had not.

And I wrote this poem for the love and companionship that I had hoped for during some of my loneliest nights, to spite this pessimistic realm.

There are so many of my detained brothers and sisters who have bled through their fingers in working for a love that never became attainable, including myself. To have someone love you unconditionally and mean it with both their words and actions to follow; has always been like a ghostly apparition here. Sure it is clear enough to see but, as you draw near enough to reach it, it's translucent compounds weaken as your intended embrace pulls straight through its foggy form like attempting to hug the air.

As daunting as it may be at times, though, defeat would appear foreign in nature. Especially when there are sites designed specifically to cater to the imprisoned populace like FriendsBeyondTheWall.com, InmateConnections.com and SeemarsSiteSurfing.com (pending) just to name a few. But in any event, this all goes back to that of our friends and families to make such contact possible in most cases.

However, imprisonment is by far cruel and unusual punishment. For if man was meant to be by himself God would not have sacrificed the rib of Adam to create Eve. Thus forth to scatter many men and women about the earth. Because of this void, I have never been so alone or have longed to smell the scent, and feel the touch of a woman—my future wife so much in all of my day. It is like an innate emptiness or that a piece of me is incomplete without her.

It is tough to be lonely. To be unable to put your guard down without the anxiety and fear of further heartache. I have never known a want as strong as companionship. Its will can sometimes be so commanding that it becomes overwhelming.

I can see a woman on television, which whom I consider to be attractive, whether it be a sitcom, movie or commercial and literally envision a life with her... Waking up to her... And us being snuggled so close that I can feel the micro heat molecules escaping her pores and merging with my own. And I am sure having to develop a relationship with fictitious characters holds the same virtue for my many brothers and sisters, as the presence of companionship is no more than an illusion here.

So ladies it is no doubt that we need you. And though some of us may not show it in a way you would deem more appropriate, we need you to be here nonetheless; to hold, to love, to cherish, and to take away the stress and drama of our lives. Many of us may lack the ability to express that but it is up to you to save us from the evil of ourselves. You are our guiding light and we need for you not to give up on us the same way we have not given up on you. I just wanted to put that in a poem. You have humbled me.

An Out-Grown Betrayal

Date: October 5, 2011

What once stood whole beating in rhapsody at the mere thought of you, now remnants remain shattered in millions of micro-shards on account of maltreatment.

Your love so raw and intense at one point was thought to stand the test of time, as it once withstood the benefits of my presence. Thus, the fruits of my labor. An incandescent flame that only proved to be lukewarm. As deceiving as a mirage.

A pain incapable of being put into words... Something you took to be so insignificant as the blades of grass beneath your feet. For in contrast, no matter how many times they're cut down or trampled on, they again rise and continues to grow, as is my person. Therefore, had it not been for you treading over my heart I would have never known my potential, strength, and will power.

We can sometimes learn our greatest lessons from the broken pieces of us. It is because of them we learn who we truly are, where we are going. Because of them we learn again to have faith, to be more evolved and understanding…

It is because of them we learn to pray, to cry, listen, and to reach out for help. And it is because of them we learn to strive for better, and lend a hand to others in need all the same.

So if someone has ever hurt you, betrayed you, or have even broken your heart, forgive them. For they assisted in you learning of grief and the importance of being cautious when giving of yourself emotionally. Although, it is said to be better to have loved than to not have loved at all.

Commentary

Like that of a sequel to "A Disturbed Utopia," I have allowed the results of that hurt to knock me off my feet, and still as a man I am able to get back up and stand. I have been acquainted with how it feels to unwanted, discarded like the trash society has made me out to be.

I have been found though, like the treasure of a grateful recipient or of a polished diamond of manufactured coal.

My head once hung low like so many of my brothers and sisters of incarceration because of the resentment, fragile bonds of kinship, and unspoken love. Even in the melee of locking in on a cell block filled with other prisoners under the authority of prejudice guards, I felt alone with my thoughts. I have missed my children, my freedom, family and luxuries of life and still do.

There is nothing more wanted by me than striving ahead with a clean slate and making something for myself and those I love. And as it would seem, no matter how many steps I took forward, I found myself back peddling just as many backward and it angered me.

But still, I wanted to heal. I learned that carrying around that sorrow had more of a psychological price than being forgiving and moving on with my life. However, it remains my belief that time does *NOT* heal all wounds, instead it makes them easier to deal with but that emotional bruise will always be there. For it takes but a mere trigger or reminder of some sort to recall such painful events to become emotionally tyrant, again. But why live beyond your means by paying such a costly price to carry around such a vengeful and bitter heart??

Life has so much more to offer in my opinion, than just moping around. And I see it every day here. Not saying we are not entitled to mourn or grieve our situation but again, there is always that someone whose predicament is a lot worse than your own. Some of my brothers and sisters behind the wall are never to come home, or are in these places and even upon release will never see the one(s) they love again.

Those very individuals wake up a little more tired of living with each passing day, not because they want to die but because they have no purpose to live.

So I see all the more reason to relish in the lessons given by life and not let bad moments become who we are. After all, s/he who can control your thinking can in turn dictate your actions, and with your actions determine your fate. So experience is not what happens to us as a people, but what we do with what has happened to us.

Missing Out On Love

Date: June 17, 2011

My Dear,

Think about how often we miss out on love. The slightest touch, the wrong stare, a misread gesture, or even the lack of perfect timing...

We can sometimes miss out on love by the wrong words being spoken, the misrepresentation of love by our own perspectives, or expectations put on the same thereof...

We can miss out on love by our inability to conform and be patient with one another. We can sometimes miss out on love by failing to take into account the importance of communication, the relevance of commitment, paying attention to even the smallest of detail, and the significance of simply being yourself...

Some people can go an entire lifetime looking for love and never find it, merely because they failed to recognize it when it revealed itself. I'm just glad that I was able to identify ours when it finally arrived....

I Love You!

Commentary

Some say that 'LOVE' is a legend of folk lore; others believe it is only a high of life when compatibly matched with your significant other. But me, I like to think that it is a force that gives life purpose, that brings about new hope for the future, for happiness and what makes us human. Without that, we are a people dead alive. Not so much in the physical sense but internally.

I have no doubt walked these prison halls and have been housed on units and saw that same look of death, and defeat in the eyes of so many of my incarcerated brothers. And it saddens me not only because I know the feeling all too well myself, but because the look also represents the quality of their outside relationships.

In contrast, I have also seen the look of happiness, contentment, and often a glossy eyed stare from those prisoners who did have outside support. They did not possess a radiant and elated look because they had not a care in the world; after having been stripped of any responsibility whatsoever, but because they found solace in family, friends, and love.

So you see, it is not just up to our spouses to bear the burden of organizing and maintaining family structure. It is up to us, our friends and family as well to ensure the upkeep of said relationships should prison ever become a factor in our lives. It is up to us as a whole to change our society but it first starts with loyalty. Loyalty to yourself and family.

While attending a college course here I once read a quote in class that reads, "The most important thing to do if you find yourself in a hole is *STOP* digging." Although the source to this statement is unknown to me, its message is as relevant and candid today as when I read it then. Let's stop digging our nation further into a ditch by unnecessary dividedness, and lets repack that excavation by coming together as a people and start looking out for one another.

I am not saying to deliberately go out and find some stranger in the streets or in prison, and devote your time and energy to him or her. But let's give 'No Man Left Behind' a whole new meaning and bring our family members, strayed loved ones back home. How would you otherwise know if you missed out on love, if you counted us out from the outset simply because of our current place of address?!

My point is, do not be so quick to overlook our being or else you may be the one professing your love of the one who got away as in "Dear Viana."

The Prying Heart of a Lonely Prisoner

Ideal Lover

Date: July 29, 2009

I often find myself in a daze wondering how I wand up in the life and arm's of someone with such qualities.

I've always thought someone of your caliber would never exist. For the strengths you posses are far beyond average and surely surpass the characteristics of your typical woman.

Truly your very being is a blessing within itself. The reason Adams sacrifice to create Eve wasn't in vain. Flawless to my highest desire. You bring light to even some of my darkest days.

Your full luscious lips, soft hands, breath-taking physique along with wits that also accommodates your stature. I am honored by your faithfulness and the dedication you put into our relationship/friendship. And for that, I feel forever in debt to you.

Deeming You *MY* Ideal Lover.

Commentary

Never will I profess to being a great poet, wordologist, or even a skilled writer. For I have even eluded studying the subject altogether in an attempt to preserve how coarse, raw, and uncut my thoughts are. Rather, I am simply blessed in being brazen enough to address my emotions and inner-most feelings. There is an age old adage that goes, a man should be the 'strong and silent' type, and that sentiments are for women. I contest that by reasoning with whatever was taken out of man to create a woman of feminine origin is a matter to be seriously considered.

Because of this there are men who are feeling emotions they have trouble verbalizing. They are hurting; they feel sad and weak inside. Subsequently, those same harbored feelings are deliberately filling so many state and federal prisons in most of the cases. Thus after having time to extend my vocabulary I sought to channel such "emotion" by expressing what I felt via pen and pad.

Inasmuch, life in prison is a daily war. You not only have to worry about other rival prisoners but the officials here as well. They are all corrupt in some shape or form. We are being oppressed, verbally abused, and beat on more times than not. And a lot of times we are the ones being provoked to react and then beaten savagely where some of us were unable to survive the attack.

It is emotionally draining and a lot of prisoners are suffering. Some of them have committed suicide and/or put themselves in an even worse predicament, right here behind these very walls where I scribe to you. Perhaps because the punitive damages associated with being abandoned, coupled by prison politics were too much to bear; or because that was the only way they knew how to convey their intended message.

That being the case, this poem was written to surmount the challenge of sharing the intimate details of my gratitude for those who allowed my voice to be heard. There was no one particular person in my life at the time it superseded the phase of being an idea and turned into a project. Not taking anything away from those who were personally invested during its development at some time or another.

However, in prison you may very well have people who will enter and leave your life. So each quality expressed therein were derived from a number of individuals who left a lasting impression on my heart. It took some time to tamp all of those feelings into one literary piece, but it was indeed the focal point of me realizing my ability to write.

Flower of Snow

Date: November 5, 2011

You flourish even in the harshest of environments. Your flushed pink lips as naturally dyed tips of pinnate-leaves.

Your beautiful alabaster skin, as smooth and soft to the touch as the fuzz atop freshly sprouted rose petals. As velvety as the crème of vanilla bean, yet as durable as the conditions of the many seasons you've weathered.

Your body as the pistil by means of having reached your maturity in a physical sense. Though psychologically, you still possess the vulnerability of a growing mind.

Your freckled face, bold green eyes, and auburn hair making an imposing display in a fallacious manner. As would a predatory plant to attract the prey of its liking. Or as harmonious as a humming bird hovering about your fragrant leaves, anticipating the flavors of your sweetly scented pollen.

Nonetheless, without its proper nutrients; it would merely be a bulb on barren ground.

Commentary

In this poem, I wanted to keep the pretense within the coordinates of a flower as I have identified mine. However, as a man it is up to you to water and nurture your own from first being a seedling, to sprouting as a bud, and becoming a beautiful flower.

We as men can sometimes get so caught up in our hardened macho lives that we neglect our duty to protect, provide, and fertilize our flower with love and care. To be mindful of her delicate vulnerabilities and the effort required in utilizing the proper gardening tools to ensure her longevity in self-assurance and character.

Naturally, like a flower, life provides a woman with all the sustenance needed to preserve life, the environment to bloom, and the necessary processes of pollination. But also, much like that of a floral arrangement, how is it that her true beauty is to be recognized without its pleasantly defined upkeep?!

So in a sense, it is us who validates who our flower is and the like; as the saying goes, "A job is no short of a self portrait of the person performing the task at hand.

In this aspect, such regard can be the expression of words possessing the same trait as 'planted seeds' in determining if they will later appear, either as a bouquet of flowers or weeds. Your spouse or mate is a reflection of you and the kindness rendered in dealing with this individual.

It is imperative that we mold our partners, not by way of physiological make-up but psychologically as our equals. A lot of times we treat our woman like the delicate flower she is, but rack our brains in frustration because she does not handle things in a manner that is appropriate to us, or because our thoughts do not accommodate each others. When indeed it was us who never gave them the nutrients to grow with us.

We will wait until we are faced with drastic situations or when things are in a complete disarray, to expect our precious little flower to have blossomed at her fullest potential I have heard the, "But I did this and that for her," story so many times that I have come to resent it just as much as I hated my son calling someone else dad. Not that I disagree with being a step-parent as I was raised by my now deceased step-father (Ronald Flynn) but because he acted as if he did not know that I was his father at all. If nothing else, this is your duty to assure your child knows who his or her parents are, if at all possible.

The same is the case with the aforementioned dilemma, because the source of it all dates back to ignorance and lack of communication. So again, we have to communicate honestly if it is ever expected of us to aid our woman in flourishing into a beautiful flower. It is how our rays of love shine down on her like that of the sun, our kind touch that hydrates the soil she grows in, and us communicating that she feeds off the victuals of our words that allows her to stand out amid any array of flowers.

However, when speaking of having 'identified' my flower, my intentions were solely to justify my preference, though not exclusive. I have not yet been afforded the privilege of caring for nor possessing such a graceful creature that I could call my own, and I'm sure for many of us here the feelings are mutual. It always appears that in our attempts to nurse our flowers, in time, they either wilt or wither away.

In writing this poem, I noticed that along the way I was describing another pen-pal friend of mine whose letter fruition was also short lived.

But in good faith, for many of my captive brothers and sisters, including myself, finding our flower is imminent and remains a declaration of our optimism.

An Understanding Beyond Words

Date: August 22, 2011

Dedicated to Samihah J.

They say that life is a precious gift. Whether it's given or taken under any circumstance is a complex process, a work of combined forces beyond human comprehension.

The same goes for a woman baring a child, coming to love someone more than your own. A selfless act that requires great patience, strength, and sacrifice all the same. All qualities of which, among others, you encompass in the form of a delicate vessel.

As beautiful as a butterfly during its metamorphose phase, to wit, the enduring of your own physical taxation. Each stretch mark and other post pregnancy disfigurement taking on the position of every radiant color, signifying its own level of appeal.

I am worthy of your devoted motherly resilience. The nurturing, caring, and teaching of another while maintaining your own development. Still a youth yourself, yet a complete compliment to the creation of mankind.

You are a magnificent woman, a true friend and I am honored that you chose to carry my/our child through life. We have had yet to grow as parents but my appreciation and love for you exceeds words. Truly I am sorry for not being able to get there sooner but just as in the title, some things don't need to be said to be understood. You already know where my heart is...

Commentary

True, by way of dedication this poetic profession was written to illustrate my respect and appreciation of my eldest son's mother. She and I are presumed to be great friends and though our communication has been strained with the years of my untimely incarceration, I wanted her to know and understand her place with me.

Not to salvage what stands to remain of our relationship, but to engage her confidence in being my life partner in parenthood. Similar to the relativity of my youngest son's mother. Neither of you are on a pedestal to high for the other, as the three (3) of us are on the roster for the same team, in which we all play a significant role in securing the win.

That is what makes it a 'TEAM,' everyone plays a part to accommodate the whole of us. You do not have to be the best in all areas of the field; you need but only specialize in trying, or in other words playing your part not to be confused with "playing the game."

In reference of such, it is not seldom for me to wear my emotions on my sleeve. Some call that a weakness and others a double-edged sword, but I like to call it exactly what it is, me. I have had dudes on more than one occasion deliberately tell me that because of such, I fail to 'play the game' or do not know how to play it in either order.

A very interesting statement is this, because I do not see the strife of my current legal matters as a "game." I do not see how anyone else could either. Waking up every day to constant confinement is not a "game," neither is not knowing my sons outside of prison. Losing my best-friend to time and family members alike, now known simply as relatives is not a "game." And neither is coming to jail in my teens and having to fathom the thought of being released well into my thirties.

These things among so many others are not necessarily subjects I take lightly. So where is this game I hear a selected few speak of? Is it in death, a broken heart, in ailment or any other association of such?! There are brothers and sisters of mine whose lives have been completely altered because of this so called "game," not to mention its effects on the children.

I know a brother on this very unit with me who have been imprisoned for over thirty (30) years and have never had one single visit. Let's think about that for a second, this man is both a father and grandfather and has been in prison for longer than most of us here have even been alive and has not seen his family, yet he remains hopeful and steadfast on one day making it back home to them.

This is precisely the purpose of this very book, to tell the story of a lonely prisoner as common as that is here. And to continue to advocate communication and rebuilding of the family structure, as is my intention on jotting said poem.

So in grasping the subtext of such, this bridge of familial interest takes priority amid any obstacle in life. It is the cornerstone of our faith, values, and what softens life's harsh edges. Being without that . or having it taken away from us, has the potential to breed discontention, which often leads to anger and ultimately aggression or violence amongst one another.

We will fight but as if we have lost our sense of direction, like being unable to distinguish between friend and foe. Be that as it may, we only have ourselves to blame in allowing one another to forget who we are. For it takes but a shift in perception to become stronger and reconstruct where we stand as family.

III

Sultry Erotica

My Imaginary Love Story

Date: August 16, 2011

Imagine my eyes starring deeply into your own. Or me engaging the electrons in your fruit supple lips, while gently pressing them against mine…

As I pause to bask in the moment before rounding your chin to trace your neck line with my kisses. Making sure to leave no part of you unsavored.

Imagine the strength of my hands being compressed along the length of your physique, caressing the contours of every unique curve on your body. Paying special attention to your more sensitive areas…

Invading the very essence of your femininity with the tip, center, and base of my tongue. Violently lapping your sweet secreting nectar, glazing the lower half of my face in the process.

Imagine me resurfacing to meet your star studded gaze, only to have my love muscle sink into your slick and creamy cavity of exultant joy. Penetrating the layers that none has yet to conquer while strategically thrusting at a controlled pace…

Our legs intertwined, as our bodies eagerly collide with one another on a quest of seeking orgasmic release. Often changing positions before tussling back into missionary style. Grinding my shaft in to the opening of your pelvic mound in a circular like motion, until I feel your inner-self contract around my girth.

Thus having manipulated a flutter of sheer pleasure to dominate your spinal column, as you lay in rapturous delight.

Imagine...

Commentary

My Imaginary Love Story came more as a challenge than anything while having another writer for a bunk mate. As I recall in my earlier writings, a lot of my work captured more of a scorned side of me. So this teasing ode represents my transformation in scribing creativity. It is because of this poem that I began to view writing as a sport and took to diversifying my crafts technique accordingly.

In as much as embracing this strategy, it enabled me to foster more of a strength in jotting my personal assertions of penology.

Still, to that extent, I will not say that I sexualize everything. But the inclusion of this chapter was necessary in that it provides clarity to a much eluded question to which I will disclose later in this section.

However, like so many of us confined brothers and sisters; even in prisons where conjugal visits are allowed or where they lack the exploitation of the privilege thereof, it is not uncommon to become more sexually deviant and/or more confident in voicing our wants via coital affairs.

Further, I had written another poem to be included as well, titled, "One Sided Pleasure," which detailed catering to the needs of your significant other with the exception of copulation. It was designed to emulate the romanticism characteristics of a selfless life-long companionship.

It goes as far as spelling out coming home to an elaborate trail of rose pedals; leading to a decorated candle lit washroom, bubble bath, and chilled Melot—pushing the boundaries of hot and cold sensations. Given the magnitude of the circumstances, the objective was apparently to provide much deserving relaxation in a sauna like atmosphere. I chose not to include it in a last minute draft, as a result of it 'telling' more than 'showing' the reader of its capabilities.

Moreover, I also toyed around with other titles appealing toward pleasing the spouse before settling on that particular one. I just took more to the grouping of those words, and not just because I am currently an avid participant in engaging in self-sex, no pun intended.

Nah' but I take pride in pleasing my woman. So 'One Sided Pleasure' may very well be utilized in another project of mine. Unfortunately, I have been incarcerated since the age of nineteen (19), so a lot of these feelings are not just an emotion but that of a simulation of the things I would like to do for my future wife.

Forever I Want

Date: January 29, 2012

To peel your clothes like the protective layers of a citrus fruit, the fuzzy sheathing of a sweet kiwi berry, or the rind of a syrupy mango melon to reveal your bare skin.

Forever I Want...

To eagerly eat you out of some edible panties, before I let you sit on my face and I drink from your fountain of life.

Forever I Want...

To in turn, have you take the fullness of me into the small opening of the warm and salivatory confines of your mouth, and suck me feverishly like that of frozen dessert in the summer's heat; but stop abruptly, before orgasm, giving me all the more reason to aggressively take you from behind.

Forever I Want...

To first allow you to ride me. Leaving your milky love to lightly coat the exposed areas of my manhood, while you hungrily lift and lower yourself onto my plump middle with force, in a crazed state of sexual bliss.

Forever I Want…

To continue to explore the many flavors of you as we exhaust the virtue of kama sutra. Then to lastly proceed in doggy-style position, as I ravish your tight and wet cunny with each wild thrust, causing your soppy juices to spill out even more. Thus, soaking my lower abdomen with that of your liquid heat until our journey of ecstasy is finally fulfilled.

Forever I Want...

To rejuvenate, for us to perpetually relive those succulent moments of animalistic lust and passion.

Commentary

One of my greatest pet-peeves is probably the stigma that follows a prisoner of homo-or-bi-sexuality. This by far, in my opinion is one of the biggest misconceptions here, that and being in prison in smooth sailing.

Do not get me wrong, there is definitely a lot of under handed weird occurrences that goes on here regarding gay jokes amongst some circles, including the participation in part on most corrections officers. The jokes can sometimes go so far as to even become offensive in nature, but homo-sexuality is not necessarily a lifestyle preserved for prisoners.

Sure there are those of they who opt to partake in such activities just as they do in society, but every incarcerated fe/male does not fly that way.

The ones that do indulge in the life of being bi-or-homo-sexual is something that has already manifested within them, either in thought or by happening to succumb to the actual act, whether they choose to come out before or after prison or continue to keep it secretive.

Not saying that I am phobia prone or to have my words conflicted and/or misconstrued as to imply that I am against gays of any sort. But I for one choose not to walk such a path. Where it is I have a problem is when these undercover bi-or-homo-sexual men engage in that life then plague unsuspecting women with various diseases and viruses. Whereas even if s/he did inform their mate or spouse of such interactions, there is NO safe way to become involved here and still protect yourself (i.e. condom or other barrier method). So any excuse as to why or how she or he did so would simply be self-serving and rendered moot.

Although I cannot account for the events that takes place at a women's institution, the same would apply for those of us prisoners who are presented the opportunity to become intimate with a civilian or other prison official. It does happen, but how are we to know what that individual does or has been exposed to in our absence?!

Another scenario that requires great consideration is returning home to a lover who have more than likely been sexually active while the other partner was away, namely by way of being detained for allegedly having committed a crime.

In this instant matter, we must be mindful of the H.I.V./AIDS clause where even if tested first, the test only goes back three (3) months prior which provides a ninety (90) day gray area. What this means is that it does not register as to whether this virus has been contacted within this three (3) month grace period before taking the test.

So as in the second verse of stanza two (2) in "I Believe," respectively we have to be responsible in our dealings as not to give virtue to the age old proverb which reads, "One night of pleasure can leave you a life of grief." So it goes both ways.

Turning back to thinking of serving hard time in the penitentiary as being a smooth sail• With a soaring recidivism rate of sixty-five (65) percent and a prison population exceeding 2.4 million in the United

States alone, it is completely understandable how one could perceive the notion that something spectacular must go on here, to keep these guys and gals coming back.

Well, one (1) thing for certain is that it is not the service received, and two (2) for sure is that a stay-cation is neither a contributing factor. Whereas in contrast, often the food is under-cooked and nowhere near edible. We are compelled to perform pain staking labor only to be under paid, while the cost of living here or the commissary prices if you will are constantly being raised.

Even in striving to better oneself, the oppression has come to a point as to insinuate that we are being punished even for seeking an education, hence the primary goal of rehabilitation. Yet it would seem the officers have made and continue to make every attempt to intimidate us, and to discourage our academic endeavors.

For example, we are only allowed to attend the provided college course(s) twice a week for a period of 2.5 hours each session, and still, the classes are regularly being called out late, thus causing the 2.5 hour time bar to be reduced to an even shorter lecture.

I have heard some officers rhetorically question aloud, "Why don't they just abolish this s*** (program)." We have been called "fake college students," while being peered down on with piercing wicked stares in an attempt to break our spirits. And in the closing weeks of our latest semester, we were advised by custody to longer carry our folders to class which contained research documents and so forth. Even before that, officers have taken and broken our writing utensils to further prevent our empowerment.

They create a troubling environment by shouting biased remarks as we cross their paths on the compound, while scurrying along to our place of study or other appointments. Recently, an area lieutenant interrupted our study group making a fuss about us using the bathroom while in class, as if it were not made for that intended purpose. In addition to our tardy arrivals, there have also been times when some tier officers would not let us out for class at all, even when it was called out over the prison P.A. system. And no one says or does anything about it because they fear retaliation.

Now, they have broken the prison down into two (2) complete sections. Either you work or you go to school, there is no in between. The problem is that with no outside support, you have to work to provide for yourself. But if you are trying to educate yourself, you will not be able to make a living here. Nothing is free, of course. So the opportunity cost is greater than the risk of simply not wanting to return to prison. But most guys have no choice other than to work.

So the prisoners that might want to better themselves are coaxed into doing otherwise. I will testify to this under oath or submit to a polygraph in attesting that in most cases; prison is *NOT* rehabilitating our brothers and sisters, but making us worst. We are so exhausted and tired that there is little to no fight left, and the ones that do fight back are considered a menace to society and treated as such.

To this truth, we are not just okay being in jail. This, in my opinion, is a concentration camp or a branch of modern day slavery where we are daunted from learning by our over-seer, who only seems adamant in forcing us to be over worked for little to no pay. Do not be duped by movies such as 'Good-Fellas' and other propaganda into believing prison folk lore about jail life. And I know there are those of you who disagree or feel that we are deserving of this treatment until perhaps circumstances, errors, or even a mistake in the judicial system mandate said roles to be reversed and it is now your son, brother, or husband, etc. to find themselves in the shoes of the man (or woman of course) in the cell next door.

I thought that would get your attention. Now picture yourself, that relative or loved one living under those same conditions for a lesser included offense outside of the underlying in, "Our Lost Brothers and Sisters," such as a misdemeanor of some sort. This is why we must make a change. The objective is far greater than just the complacency of you and me, but us as a people.

IV

Environmentally Bred

Knowing Where You Came From Is Not The Same As Being Where You Are.

Do Not Become a Victim Of Circumstance

I Believe

Date: July 15, 2011

That the basis of life is truly based on what we make it out to be.

That even as a people, you can't truly know where it is you're going, until you know where it is you've come from.

That a true friend is not the one who is always eager to stand at your side whenever trouble arises, but the one who has the heart to tell you that you are getting involved in some nonsense to begin with.

And that you can never truly lose until you give up entirely...

I Believe

That just because someone else's relationship may appear to be perfect, doesn't necessarily mean that's at all the case, or the like.

That just because a person says that they love you does not mean that very individual won't be the one to hurt you the most.

That unless you learn to love yourself completely, you cannot love anyone else.

And that to be intelligent, you do not have to win every argument. For the wise one knows when to agree to disagree...

I Believe

That as a man, my pride can sometimes hinder me from making better decisions.

That no matter how hard you try, you cannot please everyone at once.

That there are many people who act without thinking, just as there are they who think without acting.

And that it is okay to sometimes to cry in front of your children, or to not always know the answer. It shows humility and that you are only human...

Commentary

Verily the belief of any individual correlates to the development of that persons character, which defines our choices and ultimately determines the consequences we are to undergo, be it a negative or of a beneficial nature.

True to form, it is through this analogy that we discover the ability to dictate the outcome of our own destiny. As fate would have it though, often it is too late for the realization of this power to resignate within us. This becomes a commonplace for so many of us here, partly in ignorance and in another part because some just will not have things other than their own way.

Unfortunately, the ones to also suffer the ramifications of this mindset is not just the victims of our crimes but that of our families and loved ones as well.

So even in my description of the oppression in prison or in the world abroad, my problem is not with racism or how one chooses to live his or her life, but how divided we are as families.

In the "Willie Lynch Letters," it explains how the mothers' were made to watch as the men who were thought to be both the protectors and providers of women were beaten savagely. As the roles were then reversed, these women, because they feared the same would come of their sons, instinctively taught him to be weak-minded though strong physically. They then taught their daughters to be just as obedient and to raise their future sons in the same fashion.

This was called 'Sound Slave Economics' then, however, in today's post Emancipation Proclamation era is commonly known as the 'Generational Curse,' for those of us who were not given an example of what a good family is or should be for that matter.

The point is this though, we as men need to step up as well and reclaim our roles. It is time for us to break this chain of ignorance, to do away with the ideology of dysfunctional family and be the husbands, fathers, and leaders we were meant to be in accommodating the roles we require of our woman, and so forth.

It is not just the duty of our significant other to strive in bettering our financial and co-relational future. We, even as prisoners or those free must be willing participants in rebuilding the family structure. We must rid ourselves of this block boy mentality and be there to protect, provide and nurture or woman. For it is not the streets that validates who we are as a (wo)man, but the impression we leave on our loved ones and those that surround us.

Far too long women have filled the void that we men have left behind and became both mommy and daddy, nurturer and provider, and it is well deserving of them to be finally awarded a moment of rest and peace of mind. Not that this is our only route to salvation but it is a start.

We needn't worry about what has worked for someone else to achieve said liberation, but focus solely on what works for us and our family. No more, no less.

All this said to say, though this book addresses the needs of persons, primarily prisoners, who cope with abnormal conditions when separated from those that love them, by educating same on preserving family ties and exposing the naked truth of what goes on here. We must still be held accountable for the lifestyle choices that put us here to begin with. After all, how are we to learn from a mistake we never acknowledge ever making?!

The Prying Heart of a Lonely Prisoner

A Thugs Apology

Date: August 22, 2011

I was always told that a "Sorry Nigga" ain't s*** but this apology may just make a better man of me yet.

I'm sorry for all the nights I didn't come home, you sat up hoping that every time the phone rang, it wasn't some detective telling you that I'd been found lying unresponsive on one of these city blocks.

I'm sorry that I disregarded your hopes and dreams for me, allowing my street life to supersede family obligations.

I'm sorry for all the decisions I made that not only put my life in danger, but that of those I love(d) as well.

Here and now, from the depths of my soul, I apologize...

I'm sorry for all the letters you had to write following my incarceration, and all the energy you put into coming to visit me in the different jails and prisons I've resided in over the years.

I'm sorry for all the times I wasn't there as a man to protect and shelter you from the hardships and temptations from both this world and its wrongdoers.

I'm sorry for all the lies I've told, not having taken responsibility for why I wasn't around to help raise my sons.

Here and now, with this pledge of sincerity, I apologize...

I'm sorry for all the times I brought my problems home, using you both mentally and physically as a mechanism to vent and release my own pent up tensions.

I'm sorry for the attempts on my life that left you traumatized for ages to come.

I'm sorry that my absence left you susceptible to making sacrifices that you wouldn't otherwise have to make just to get by, had I been there.

Here and now, please believe me, I apologize...

Commentary

A steady drizzle of many emotions becomes either a man or woman compelled to forgo captivity. Among them are usually anger, remorse, and/or self—engineered disappointment, etc., etc. For me, at this point a struggle began from within regarding right and wrong—peace and chaos—life or death.

It is obvious which route I chose. But there are many of us who remain undecided as to what path to follow, and as such, this battle for self continues inside of them. It is not that they are unable to distinguish between either two or are unwilling to change for the better, but this life is all a lot of my brothers and sisters here know.

Can you even imagine the grief of these stricken men and women? A grief that need not any clarity. For it is written on their faces; in their eyes you see the first signs of defeat though their overall appearance holds true to strength, and the aggression exuded.

Often we as prisoners are misjudged by the manner in which we choose to live, when indeed the inability to modify a way of life most are a product of is as complex as breaking the custom of addiction. Respectively, an addiction is any over-indulgence that compromises the 'Free Will' of said addict. The similarities are close knitted in that they both harness a lifestyle change. And like any addictive, you must be patient and endearing as the sobriety phase is attempted.

Nevertheless, this apology originates there from my deepest found sorrow and is particularly for my mother and everyone that has not turned their backs on me over the years. It is for all those who have been affected by my reign in the streets in any way, as well. For it was in this state that I had succumbed to my own dependency issues. Not so much as in the sense of indulging in narcotics or any other intoxicant, but in my addiction of acquiring a hasty financial gain by making unworldly decisions.

Additionally, it is also within my reach to extend this apology to my sons. It is through you two (2) that I have found a purpose in all of this, my means to realign my perception on life. I love you beyond any recognizable definition of the term and I am so very proud to be your father. Thank you for creating the detour that revealed the pathway to my detoxification in relieving myself of both my once poisonous heart and state of mind.

Friend or Foe

Date: October 4, 2011

They swear to be of your best interest when indeed they are truly not. A foe can appear in many forms... One can show as a lover, a relative who is a friend of someone else, or even as your own child(ren) seeking to fill your shoes.

They can reveal them true selves after years of friendship, a short term commitment, or even a lifelong companionship.

They swear to be with you during both the bitter and the sweet when surely they lie. For if that tartness was to supersede the flavors more appeasing to the tongue, very few would be able to stomach the taste. They may very well at first do have the best of intentions, but overall we are merely human.

Should that same mortal weakness then not render a punishment of some sort? Or is it equally punishable as it also evokes betrayal, disloyalty, and disappointment all the same.

They say that we are too sensitive or the fools for taking such heartache so seriously. Are we then those of the losers for believing in genuine beings, or for feeling like we deserve better from those who put on a charade and mask themselves as someone familiar.

It is said that in this life we are entitled to maybe one true friend, and that the chances of finding him or her are next to none. With that as a variable, in our encounter which will you be...

Friend or Foe

Commentary

I have never felt so trapped by life and isolated from love and true fellowship than I do at this very moment.

I hate that while in route, you cannot even be genuine in your transactions with the individuals you encounter along the way. Because in turn, you later come to find out that very person had some mean twist or hidden agenda in fraternizing with you to begin with.

There is so much hopelessness and trickery that surrounds us prisoners, that I feel like I am being choked by bitterness. And that with each gasp for air I can feel my youth, happiness, and innocence leaving my body; as if I were an asphyxia victim on his or her last dying breath.

I feel restricted from life itself and that no one understands my struggle to live.

I feel behind in time and that everyone else has moved on without me... That it is just me holding on to the times when it was safe to love and be a friend... When death was only thought to prevail in old age and sickness was but some hot soup, Children's Tylenol and mothers love away from a cure.

Today that love has reached an inferior state; at least where I come from, anyway. This also corresponds to a countless number of my imprisoned brothers and sisters alike. A place where friends are murdered and often by each other. Where the Victim(s) Impact Statement involves his or her mother explaining a time of having to feed you when yours could not. Where getting up with childhood buddies or buddettes, you find out that s/he's completely someone else. The smiles, jokes, and laughs are the same and the handshakes, hugs, and love have the same feel but the intentions are centered on greed or other matters associated with ill-will.

Sometimes it is too late to discover that you are a friend of an enemy, more commonly known as a *frenenemy*. Surely each of these may appear in many a form, but in my own personal dealings, coming to this realization can sometimes be a great feat in liberation and in others, can hurt more than a divorce proceeding and you wish you had not found out at all. So often this note of disdain can grow into something more destructive.

Notwithstanding, a friendship can inevitably reach this devastating impasse by the same descriptive manner written in, "Missing Out on Love." But in all actuality, it all boils down to paying attention to detail and knowing who it is you are dealing with.

A lot of times, we can speed through life and miss the many tell-tale signs that could have very well forewarned of the events to come. For example, we know that in being deceitful; a tell-tale sign would be that lie possibly coming back to bring more harm than it initially being told..Or if you know of someone who is a shady businessman and/or associate; the tell-tale signs are the flak or breach in trust that may very well follow in dealing with this person.

It is not always this simple, but we must be just as meticulous as we face life's twist and turns. If not, what an evil destination there is to come.

Loyalty is...

Date: November 11, 2011

Loyalty is... First being true to one's own self before making a commitment to anyone else. Having the courage to say when enough is enough; that you refuse to settle for less and/or when you can be honest even when it isn't to your own benefit.

Loyalty is... Not as simple as what's being said but more so about what's being done. Not having to ask for assistance before the task at hand is settled and when s/he doesn't have to voice their need for you because you're already there.

Loyalty is... When you don't have to second-guess the intentions and/or actions of those closest to you. When even in the face of doubt you can rest assured knowing that you don't have to question as to whether your associates will have your back like that of a spinal cord or not.

Loyalty is... When being self-absorbed describes your character even less with each passing day. When making a decision you not only consider yourself, but the very individuals you care about as well.

Loyalty is… When your happiness also involves the elation of those you hold dear. When your accomplishments compliment the ones you love and/or condone all the same.

Loyalty is… Being devoted to your craft and being both faithful and mindful of the words you speak.

Loyalty is… When you value your friendships, business associates, and family ties equally. When you genuinely care about those in your circle, accept their vices, and respect them in a non-judgmental way.

Loyalty is… Tending your responsibilities as a man; providing shelter, protection, and/or financial support to your dependents. When you can support their ideas, aspirations, and goals.

Loyalty is… When you can wholeheartedly encourage their dreams, plans and console them in times of failure, too.

All these things describe what loyalty means to me, but in essence, what does it mean to you?

Commentary

Loyalty is not what it says but rather what it indeed does. It amazes me how so very few people understand this connotation yet the term is so loosely utilized by many.

So it goes, as in "Friend or Foe," this is how the innocence or perhaps the feeling of being in over your head can be misinterpreted as betrayal. Whereas, if a vow of loyalty becomes evoked under any circumstance, whether you did or did not intend for said testament to be tested or taken to such an extent can be viewed as a serious matter. Even if this act was taken out of context by the individual on the receiving end of said comment.

This is another example why communication is so important. Because in the absence of such, public opinion, storms of rumor and innuendo will fill the gap. Either you communicate effectively or others will do so for you.

I believe this is a lesson many of us fail to take heed to, including that of my co-defendant and me. In our travels in life it is too early on that we come to fall victim to allness or in other words, the erroneous belief that one embodies all there is to know about anything. This very inclination, preventing anyone else from ever telling us anything, has been the wrecking-ball in the destruction of so many relationships abroad, yet it remains an enigma among us.

Nevertheless, in falling for anything be it not your word than what there else is left to stand on. A lot of times it is our own doing that we feel cheated in our dealings with others. What I mean by this is that, in naiveté, we tend to take things for face-value and thus appraise them as such. This can often be a costly error in that a miscalculation in judgment can later present the same results in gambling, but with your life. The odds are always stacked up against you.

Incidentally this becomes problematic in how that disappointment affects the psyche. It could in turn cause you to be more conniving yourself, or even worst develop trust issues which in turn creates a vicious cycle.

All of the above further represents how easily it is for things to be wrongly perceived or over-stood. Be it something as little as a disagreement or as dramatic as larcenous greed. So again, loyalty should not be told or written. In that, what are words when deeds say so much more?

Our Lost Brothers and Sisters

Date: November 13, 2011

So many times, too often, we are losing the lives of our brothers and sisters in the viciousness of these streets.

Is it that in today's society, a life is valued in equivalence to the very bullets that bring them to an end. The bottle of alcohol you purchased and consumed before getting behind the wheel. The narcotic trip you partook before waking up oblivious to the stolen life, taken the previous night. Or having overdosed and not been able to wake up at all.

Whatever the purpose to kill; whether it be centered on vengeance, desire or happen to be accidental. Our children are growing up in single family homes, and in most cases, without parental supervision whatsoever.

As a result, the streets are raising our babies into becoming the villains we once enjoyed in cartoons as youth. While prisons and violence at the hands of one another are claiming the fathers; and promiscuous sex, drugs, and the benefits of this material world are claiming most mothers.

Partly because the fathers are gone, and without a legacy left behind to set an example for the women to follow. A detrimental impact that causes the majority to lose a sense of themselves, as they no longer value their self-worth or morals; out of ignorance in another part.

Sociologically, today's youth have been to more funerals than weddings... At this rate of crime, how much longer will it take before we completely lose our identity in continuing to contribute to this cycles repetition—when will it end??

Commentary

I wrote this poem as a tribute to our fallen loved ones, and those of us who love them. I felt that it had been warranted in the sense that, if the masses are not awaken this reality, how will we ever progress.

Recovery first starts with identifying the problem, as in every therapeutic program. In our case, we must first be willing to admit ourselves in receiving treatment to begin with.

Like so many of us though, imprisoned or not, I have lost a number of close associates and loved ones to senseless violence. I cannot begin to detail the pain of a parent who has had to bury a child, but I do understand the anguish of the lost as described in, "Voices of Silence."

It is as if this has become our normal national tone of speech. And because of it our mothers are outraged and dying inside, where each newly marked grave tells the story of another family submerged by grief.

We are always so eager to mouth that s/he who is not with me is against me, or to declare someone else an adversary... But indeed it is until we realize that the true enemy to have emerged is from within our own selves, will we ever make a change. In this assessment, we must then redirect the distribution of our anger and aggression into the formation of something more constructive. As simply identifying the problem will not provide a remedy of said epidemic.

Moreover, in referring back to the letter of 'Willie Lynch,' it further narrates, "By killing of the protective male image and by creating a submissive dependent mind of the nigger male savage, we have created an orbiting cycle that turns on its own axis forever, unless a phenomenon occurs and reshifts the positions of the male and female savages."

A savage defines us as an untrained people, and in many respects it would appear this way. We hunt and murder one another as if we are the squanderers of life or that we ourselves are an item on the food chain. Notwithstanding a race barrier of any sort, it is in us where this phenom lies.

Throughout my nine (9) plus years of travel behind the wall, nearly every brother that has been encountered by me has expressed remorse at some time or another, including myself. It is in our every prayer that we seek repentance, ask to be forgiven, hope for another chance and request that our loved ones are protected from the same inhumane acts. For, had it been revealed earlier on that the events to follow our choices would come to alter the psychological state of our women, children and the way our communities operate. I assure you this result would not be the case.

To that end, however, for many of us, expecting the worse has become second nature. This is precisely why it is so easy for us to expect negative motives in others. In turn, we are thus given a generalized misgiving and distrust among one another which develops a sense of ghost-enemies. What this means is that in thinking defensively, we can sometimes make an enemy for ourselves that would not otherwise exist.

In giving each other the benefit of the doubt, we create healthier relationships amongst our people and thus, immobilize this increasing rate of violence in our lives.

V

A Family Torn at the Seams

A House Divided Cannot Stand Against Itself

-Abraham Lincoln-

My Grandmother's Portrait

Date: June 21, 2011

Dedicated to Deborah H.

Caught in the moment, captured by the presence of sheer beauty.

The scenery resembles shades of metallic and smoke gray, varying in tint. Unconventional to ones perception of what embodies the term. Though naked to the untrained eye, unmistakably evident.

Plastered onto the canvas of this sight reveals years of uncertainty, struggle, and pain. Abused by the strife of attempting life's twist and turns, yet settled by the strength of survival innately learned.

Strong for the ability to endure, but weak from its mortal compounds all the same. Vulnerable yet unbreakable. Intelligent through wisdom by trial and error but grounded by receptiveness.

Despite, still dangling somewhere between life and my own utopia, in a trance like state... I find myself slowly coming back to reality, noticing that all along I was looking at an image of my grandmother's younger self in an older portrait.

What Beauty?!

Commentary

Throughout the totality of the English Dictionary, there are no words, yet invented to depict what 1 feel for my grandmother. She is a remarkable woman and it is such an honor to be of her acquaintance, let alone her spawn. The world would indeed be a better place, if there were but, more inhabitants like her in it.

My grandmother has been my friend, mother, confidant and advisor among other things, even when no one else would, to say the least. She has thus far been my provider, have given me strength, and guidance when all else seemed lost and turbulent times appeared to get the better of me.

So I wrote this poem as a token of my appreciation, and to capture her own unyielding strength in a literary sense.

The idea was inspired by a black and white photograph of R&B songstress Robyn "Rihanna" Fenty—courtesy of GQ Magazine, January/2010 issue. It reminded me of an older picture back home consisting of the same grades, and as I considered the beauty of such, it became clear that her character was well worthy of note.

However, one of the hardest lessons we must learn is knowing which bridge to cross and which bridge to burn. I am of a selected few to have such a strong-willed and caring woman to stand at my side and have my back during these trying times, as she is a rare specimen.

I recall a time or two literally sobbing to my grandmother via telephone, regarding my disappointments and hurt of outside irritations, following my incarceration and her consoling me accordingly. She has been there for me from the time of my arrest, up to this very moment and I am internally grateful of her.

So again, I believe that all prisoners have been a victim of verbal or some other abuse, while imprisoned by the very people who normally would not act or speak to you as such on any other occasion. One moment in particular, my grandmother would do three-way calls to enable my ability to contact persons who could not allow me to call collect. And though it was on her dime, I had not realized then, that if it was of necessity for said individuals to have heard my voice, they would very well have made the attempts to create the possibility of such.

Furthermore, this incident involved an argument between my youngest sons mother and me, usually behind the nature of our relationship and my lengthy sentence. However, she having said some foul and uncharitable things to me before hanging up the phone; cutting our conversation short even before the provided time had actually expired. I had not been able to get back through to her line for the remainder of the night. I then explained to my grandmother that I would call again the following week, and it is presumed that she noticed my being upset even though neither of us ever mentioned it.

Upon doing so, by three-way calling of course, her initial greeting was, "You be telling your grandmom my business?" I denied the accusation and she then gave me the run-down on how my grandmother called to confront her on the manner in which she had spoken to me the previous week, who later confirmed the story.

It is not a rarity for my grandmother to take liberties of this sort, mandating both letters and visits from relatives whenever possible. But it should not be under forced will that these events should take precedence, especially if you profess to care for this person.

Many of my brothers and sisters will never know an unconditional love to this extent, while imprisoned though.

It could be a result of their own doing by past actions put forth but there is always room for growth.

It bothers me that we can put on this image and act as if we ourselves are without flaw, have never made a mistake, or needed time to grow before .proceeding forward. And it is aggravating because only those who have foregone what I have been through emotionally, knows how important family support is. It is within the adage of, "Let he who is without sin cast the first stone," that we should practice forgivingness.

Pain of my Mother

Date: December 15, 2011

As I unite the lids to my organs of sight and the world fades to black, I can re-visualize the anguish inscripted over the face of my mother, as her eyes are glossed with tears and I am escorted out of the court room in handcuffs.

The image appears hazy in nature, but the outcry of her internal torment is still vivid in my mind's abyss.

Though she has not been invested; for years I have known of this truth, of her agony... Of her disappointment and the resentfulness of being incapable of changing the conditions in surviving the imprisonment of her only son.

Never will I fully understand how one could be so emotionally distant, yet so compassionate and moved all at once. A baffling show of innate motherly instincts that momentarily contends all previous actions.

Thus revealing rays of love within the cracks of a crumbling hardened facade, at least that much I understood and am beyond remorseful in all the pain I caused. I love you!

Commentary

Mother, my earth, I have often wondered if it was because of your history with men that you felt unable to bond with me. If because of such, you felt that I would eventually leave or hurt you too.

One of the most haunting memories I have as a child is when we were living on Hummock Avenue in Atlantic City, New Jersey. I must have been maybe four (4) or five (5) years of age, and I remember you being entangled in a domestic dispute with your then abusive lover.

The two (2) of you were both interlocked in each other's arms when I walked in from the other room. And though you were holding your own, you requested that I go get help—namely the landlord, and I froze up because he counter ordered that if I had complied I would be subject to a whopping. Fearing the same, I just stood before you and stared on.

I have never forgotten the way you looked at me that very moment. Since then, I have often relived different scenarios on how I should have reacted to the situation, and how I would protect you today or any woman I become involved with should another man raise a hand at either of you.

You have worked extremely hard to afford my sisters and me a better life since then, and in doing so, the opportunity cost, I believe is not having established a. relationship with me.

Consequently, that emptiness coupled by the earlier years of my life consisting of a fatherless childhood, I have often been driven by blind emotion. This is not an attempt to out-source the responsibility of my irrational behaviors, or why I became so involved with the women I loved, but because I sought the affections of you in them. It is not that I despised you and/or were unproud of you that I allowed other mother figures to enter my life, but because they provided a love that I felt you did not.

Still, you birthed my life and I will love you beyond its expiration date. There is absolutely no equivalence in that of my regard for you, and in spite of the resentment to our detached and uncolorful past, all that I am is you and all that I strive for is us.

Like some of the brothers here I know, many of them would go as far as traverse the depths of hell if given only half a chance to see their mothers once more.

So if ever I have made you feel unworthy of my love or undeserving of my respect—you are. If ever I have made you feel that I was at all ashamed or ungrateful of you—forgive me. And if ever I have seemed too proud to become emotive from missing you or being without your love—I am not.

Thus our time apart is merely a stepping stone. So rather than see it as an unjust hardship, view it as me being away at a more restrictive university, to in turn, prepare and equip myself with the much needed tools in life to become a productive member of society and our future.

Role Model, Lost

Date: January 1, 2012

At a loss for words, as I try to recount the history we share, if any at all.

Empty thoughts of a beloved stranger is all I can summon while starring into space with opaque eyes, as if to brain storm, but nothing comes to mind.

No wait; alas, something surfaces but remains faint as if to struggle to stay a memory. Maybe if I strain just a little harder, I can hold it long enough to verbalize what I see.

Damn, just you aggressively handling a lady friend of yours... It's gone. Now just years of my sisters and me at grandma's. F***, more years of— Oh, there you go. A familiar face but I can't quite put a name to it... RUN and my small body do as my mind says. Gone again, too fast.

Hold up, I knew I could think of something else... Nah' just more years of my sisters and me, only now they also include my mother this time. Hmmm, I remember that... Good times. I knew I would be able to catch back up to you again. Mom always said that I was a go getter just like you.

Wait, I feel a dark cloud coming, like things are once again turning gloomy without you. Where are you going...? I lost him again, but I still love you!

Commentary

When I wrote this poem, in my head, I envisioned myself running through the vast confines of my mind looking for lost memories of my father. Like a frantic mother in a home of a thousand (1,000) doors, in search of her lost child. Each one representing the desperation she felt, for every door opened that her child was not there.

Fortunate enough, during my twenty-nine years (29) years of life, I recall only seeing my father three (3) times. The first memorable image was that of him being abusive to his then girlfriend, I must have been between the ages of five (5) and six (6). The incident goes as follows:

Going back as far as I can remember, the three (3) of us were walking to my father's house. How we began this journey remains a mystery to this day, but I know as we walked, I explained to my father that the carry-along or over-night bag was too heavy (as I apparently was suppose to stay the night with him) and he delegated the duty of carrying such to his companion; instead of taking the responsibility himself. She objected the task stating, "You carry it, he's your son," or something to that effect. This triggered his hostile temperament, where he then violently yoked and slammed her against the nearest wall, by where we stood. The look of defeat on the face of this woman after the encounter remains a trademark for abuse in my mind's eye.

Following that situation, I remember watching television on the living room floor of my now deceased great grandmothers' (Ellen Woodall) and looking at celebrities I thought resembled my father, though I only had a fuzzy memory of his face. I sat wishfully thinking that maybe they were him and became elated with being able to see this man I hoped was my father. I also remember crying for my father there immensely for no apparent reason at all, and my mother telling me that I simply had 'Daddy Blues.' She further explained that she would eventually take me to see him, but never did.

The second time I ever saw my father was about three (3) or four (4) years later. I was either eight (8) or nine (9) years old and he came over to my grandmother's (Deborah H.) to see me, as he was suppose to had been recently released from jail, I assume. However, when he entered the living room... Spiritually I knew that we were of some relation but still, I ran upon making eye contact with this stranger. It was not because I had disliked or was disappointed in him but because I did not know who he was. My father.

117

The third and last time I saw my father was in the year of 2001 and I was at the age of sixteen (16). I was especially happy to see him this particular time because the two (2) previous visits lasted up-wards of a couple hours to a day as I recall. This visit though, was to exhaust a two (2) to three (3) week period, where my uncle Karim would later explain that we had so much in common we were unable to tolerate each other. In fact, the opposite was true and as our personalities clashed, I came to realize why my mother had kept us apart to begin with. I was on my way back home soon thereafter.

This is why the same sex role model is so important in the life of a young man growing up. It is how we become conscience of who we are and the manner in which we bond with one another. Otherwise, if we have never been given an example as to how we should conduct ourselves amongst others, we leave a void perhaps too great for reconciliation. So even if you are separated from your child(ren) for whatever reason, still reach out if possible. It will make all the difference in the long haul.

In any event, before coming to prison I was no more than a willow's wisp of a boy. But as a man before my father on solid ground and with sound mind, I can say that though I love you infinitely, because of those distant intervals between visits; I do not know how to be a son to you, but I am willing to try and that's what matters most.

On the other hand, so many of my brothers and sisters feel, or are

118

under the impression that it is better to love their child(ren) from afar due to character blemish, or what have you. But nothing can be further from the truth. On the contrary, rather, any male-human can become a father but it takes no more than a *man* to be a dad, which moves to mold the making of our days to come.

This in itself provides a direct link for parents who are 'absentee' role models, and the behavior exhibited by our youth in today's society. For example, I remember speaking with an uncle of mine some time back, regarding visitation support and so forth. It is not absolutely clear what shifted the conversation to this point, but I vividly recall him explaining that, "Because I spent more time with another relative that I should ask him (that relative) to come visit me instead."

Now suppose I had not known any better and taken that statement for face-value, and implemented it as such. This would constitute the same 'destructive' effects as me telling my sons that even with my incarceration, since you've spent more time with your mother I no longer bear the burden of being your father. It does not matter that the relationship between such 'relative' and me only accommodated our way of living at that time, and not favoritism. This man was still my mother's younger brother—like I would no doubt, still be the father of my children. And though he has not been a father figure to me, this is the type of example being set for us young men and women alike. And it's sad because my uncle too, has grown up without his father being an active figure in his life.

We come from ignorance, so often the route we choose is of the same origin. But indeed, as no one is perfect, it does not take the superior man to get involved and change this dynamic. For it takes but a unifying perspective and simply being there to make a difference in a child's life, who will come to shape the outcome of our future.

A Letter to my Sons

Date: October 25, 2011

My Princes,

Do ardently believe in your own artistic ideas and creative visions, but understand that you will often times find yourselves faced with adversity, discouraging moments, and times when you may even question your own intentions in bringing that vision to life.

You may very well find yourselves among individuals who will try to repress your dreams, who will no doubt try to asphyxiate the air you breathe, or at the very least despise you simply for being you. My sons, despite having to wrestle with coming into your own and steadying the path of your choosing, do embrace the guidance of those you trust and respect. They will aid you throughout your times of uncertainty.

Never be afraid to out-grow your friends and associates. For, sometimes it is they who will stagnate your growth both intentionally and unintentionally and, other times it will be your very own selves.

Therefore, be mindful of the decisions you make and the people you choose to surround yourselves with. With that, your thoughts can easily become your actions and your actions a habit.

Know that you don't always have to fit in to be accepted. As some of the world's greatest leaders today were at first taken as an outcast. However, do not be too proud to seek assistance; provided that is the case.

Do preserve your integrity, what sets you apart, and the unique way you view life's obstacles. Know that it is okay to be angry at times, and that it is okay to be different from everyone else; that's originality. Do believe in love at first sight, that's the origin of optimism.

And last but not least, never allow anyone or anything to drive a wedge between the two of you. There are many lessons that I would like to pass on, but surely it is a wealth too great for a single sheet of loose leaf. So in the mean time here's...

A Letter to my Sons

Commentary

Also inspired by the same bunk mate who encouraged me to pen, "My Imaginary Lore Story." Unfortunately, I had not written it in his presence so it was not contended by the critique of said person, whose opinion I valued.

Furthermore, it was prompted by a question of his similar to the effect of, "If you were on your death bed and/or were only permitted to tell your sons one last thing, what would it be?"

Without a second-thought, I mouthed with great pride and dignity, "To stick to the script and never be a sell-out," apparently referring to the blueprint of Seemars. Disapproving of my answer he then explained that my response consisted of two (2) demands and was subsequently flawed. This required me to then rethink my reply as he carefully watched my agitation liven gloatfully, as his address to such was already considered and quite timely.

However, as baffling as it was to do away with my self-satisfying retort, I asked to what might be his own solution to this conundrum. Surprisingly he simply uttered, "Read my book." This book, having been a self-help project, containing a compilation of wise quotes and life lessons. I nodded in agreement, though I had not yet thought of how I would convey a message of equal meaning, as neither of my intended books attributed to such.

Even more so, I wanted "A Letter To My Sons" to also express that of my love for them and to give the advice needed to produce a synergistic union between the two (2).

Moreover, it is not unlikely for my many brothers here, or even sisters to want to be parents and/or better examples for their children. Some will never be granted this opportunity, and for those of us who still have a chance to make a difference; a lot of times the partner-parent becomes a human blockade making that connection even less of a possibility. I wanted "A Letter to My Sons" to surpass this obstacle accordingly.

As such, a man's changing point can arise at any moment in his life, mine was the day I knew of you two (2). So coming to prison was like losing something very valuable and precious to me. Not my freedom or anything associated with it but you. You two (2) alone have been very dear to me since I first laid eyes on either of you.

It was then I realized that I wanted more out of life for both you and your mothers. It was merely an idea then, but today is surely insights for the many tomorrow's to come. I love you.

Voices of Silence

Date: January 1, 2012

The role of a father has long been recognized in the history of man. Nonetheless, whenever the topic of "Abortion" arises, a father's rights diminish to next of none.

Now of those fixated on this 'short personal essay,' I am sure a number of you are familiar with the term, or have had firsthand experience with some of the benefits of abortion.

However, there are those of us who have also experienced some of its negative effects in regard to (medical complications, etc. and) being pro-family such as myself.

In 1976 the Supreme Court held that a father has NO right over child in womb. The law was again up-held by the Supreme Court in 1988 and continues to reign this very day.

What this tells us about America is that we are not as free as we propose to be. I mean, how can this be 'The Land of the Free' when fathers who are against abortion are compelled to stand-by while their children are murdered in cold blood.

I reiterate this because an abortion does not make a woman un-pregnant; it makes her the mother of a dead baby.

Consider this: Women have had a long up-hill battle in striving for "Equal Rights" in voting, "Equal Rights" in pay, and "Equal Rights" in the work environment to name a few. But when it comes to a woman's right to choose, they opt to be a separate entity, thus contributing to a double standard.

My take on all of this; is that if, a father also equally participated in the conception process, and has to share equal responsibility in raising the child whether he chooses to or not, he then should have equal rights in the decision on whether to abort or not. And until this is dealt with justly...A father's voice is never fully heard.

Commentary

This short personal essay is dedicated to my unborn (aborted) child, as well as the many parents with whom have withstood the same. You are not alone.

I am not against abortion though. Rather, I am more inclined to advocate a fathers rights in coalition with the mothers, regarding whether or not to birth life into this world. This issue is a sentimental one for me being a father whose voice was ousted in the decision making process.

I felt silenced, like a shock collar was applied to my neck in teaching me to unlearn speech.

To this day I am deeply moved whenever I ponder the details over the loss of you, my aborted child. One moment in particular, entailed me lying in my cell listening to "*Zion*," a track from the *Mis-education of Lauren Hill* album by Lauren Hill. And I love(d) the carrying woman so, that I was still prepared to attend this sad and non-wanted event in support of her.

Some twist of fate had it that my private line was disconnected the day of the procedure. So I was unable to follow through as intended. I have moved on since then, as did she, but I have never recovered from this wound.

Nevertheless, my child, your person-hood is not forgotten nor have you perished in vain. I apologize for being neglectful and less than assertive of my parental duties. I did not fight for you the way I should have, if only I knew then what I know now, but surely you were too good for the evil of this wretched earth.

You now reside with loved ones and some good friends of mine on the other side. I know for sure they will look out for you as they once did me. And in spite of you watching over us, I wanted to tell you that you have both an older and younger brother, to wit: Ja'marion and Basim. Keep watch of them while I am away. Until we meet, I look forward to witnessing your smile for the first time. You remain a part of me forever, and now the world knows what that feels like.

VI

My Promise to a Brother

The Prying Heart of a Lonely Prisoner

"Take A Sip"

Today we as a nation—we stand at a cross roads of truth

and untruth.

Those fortunate are sure of getting water

and feel no thirst for death.

Just as the realtors of knowledge are many—

but it's understanders are few.

We are visitors to this world—and many of us

fail to realize that we cannot remain here forever.

"Untitled"

I acquaint myself with evil—not for evil

but to avoid it.

The Prying Heart of a Lonely Prisoner

Whoever does not know the evil

is deserving of falling into it.

By: Khalil "K.F." Gordy

Epilogue

It was necessary for me to write this book because I felt that I had something to say conducive to the betterment of our communities. Today we live in an environment where violent offenses are at an all time high and the urge to commit these albeit acts seems paramount to normal.

I wanted to reach out to those, especially our youth, involved in illegal activities and let them know what it means to be in prison and why it is not worth the consequences it inflicts on our people. It has become my goal to educate our families and loved ones why it is important for us to communicate and not give up on one another.

There are so many imprisoned men and women, young and old, who feel they have no voice and/or that no one understands their struggle and they feel closed in. The same goes for our youth, we have lost touch and it is as if we do not know how to relate to each other.

We as a people tend to judge by what we see, without first getting to know the source of the problem. It is similar to opting not to read a book simply because of its exterior design. We appear to be these vile and insensitive individuals but without a moment's notice, many of us would indeed retract the actions that initially brought us to this very instance.

Our youth are being misguided, as we once were. So I have taken all that I have been through to expose the truths about crime before it even reaches this end.

Therefore, my story was written to encourage self-awareness and to be utilized as therapy to strengthen identity and purpose. It is further intended to alert the generations before me and those to come, that you will face difficulties in life with your family, spouse, friends, and so on. But this does not make you indifferent or an outcast. You can still be heard, you need but speak up.

It is not expected of you alone to uphold society's standard of morality and uprightness. Rather, it is up to us as a people to mutually strive to produce a positive social environment where our youth may grow with constructive and practical views and concepts.

Everybody has struggles—some are more differed than others but regardless of such, these challenges can be surmounted. I am in the process of overcoming the odds myself; and if I can do it, so can you. Be inspired!

Thank You For Reading My Book

About the Author

Basim Reid 29, is both an aspiring author and entrepreneur. Born in America, native of Atlantic City, New Jersey where he currently resides within the N.J. Department of Corrections, serving a 15 year sentence under N.E.R.A. (No Early Release Act). There he forcibly discovered the power of writing after harbored feelings consequently led him to being housed in a number of state institutions along the way. The father of two and only son to a single mother began his 85% term of approximately 12 years in April of 2005. Since then he has made every attempt possible to reform his life and establish himself within the coordinates of the small business world.

Accomplishments While Incarcerated
At Time Of Book

Educational:

- G.E.D./High School Diploma (Standard Score Total: 2770)

Vocational Training:

- Introduction to Voc. Shops (72 Hours)

- C.O.R.E. Curriculum

- Building Trades (120 Hours)

- Carpentry Level One: Fundamentals

- Core Curricula

- N.C.C.E.R. Card (No.: 6952129)

Transitional Services/Therapeutic:

- Palm Project (Street Smarts Health Ed.)

- H.O.P.E. (Helping Offenders Parent Effectively)

- M.R.T. (Moral Reconation Therapy)

- Cage Your Rage

College; Mercer County Community College:

- English Comp, I 101 (Grade: A/Credit: 3)

- Business Mathematics 103 (Grade: A/Credit: 3)

- Speech: Human Comm. III (Grade: B+/Credit: 3)

- Principals of Marketing (Grade: A-/Credit: 3)

- Office Accounting (Grade: A-/Credit: 3)

How To Contact the Author

Please write

If you have indeed found this book useful as to obtaining a better understanding of prison life and/or feel that I have left something out relevant to you that you would like to know, or would simply like to get to know me as a person, feel free to contact me at the address below. If I cannot answer your concern(s) adequately, I will do my best to refer you to someone who can.

Additionally, as it is not uncommon for, multiple keen minds to independently come up with the same ingenious ideas or discoveries. If anyone believes that my poetry or essay's are similar to that of other creations or you know of anyone who has infringed on any of the work thereof, please contact me immediately. I have a strict policy to remove *ALL* infringing material.

Source: Entrepreneurs Guide To patents, trademarks, trade secrets, & licensing. Jill Gilbert.

Basim Reid, Sr. #566722/366104-C

South Woods State Prison

215 Burlington Road S.

Bridgeton, New Jersey 08302

URL: NJDOC.com, FriendsBeyondtheWall.com, Facebook

Other Books By The Author

Basim Reid returns with a searing and intriguing new novel based on a true story about two friends whose friendship is compelled to challenge betrayal, a possible life sentence, revenge, and most of all GREED. Don't miss this semi-memoir as it uniquely unfolds in a way that only Basim Reid can tell it!

"A BROTHER'S GREED"
Dreaming Awake

Coming - soon

Turn the page for a special preview...

A Brother's Greed

A BROTHER'S GREED
Dreaming Awake

A Brother's Greed

Chapter 1

"Hello," Eryn answered in a sensual tone after a few short rings.

"Hey girl, where you at?" Asked Jesenya.

"On my way to the parking garage at the Cherry Hill Mall. I had to run some last minute errands to make sure that everything was in line for Bashan," exclaimed Eryn.

"So he's finally about to come home, huh?" Asked a curious Jesenya. She knew how excited her friend Erin was about Bashan's return to society, after the last four years she invested into staying at his side. She had even taken a few long-ass trips up-state alongside her to visit him.

"Yeah I know. Tomorrow couldn't come quick enough either," responded Eryn.

"Mmm-Hmm," Jesenya sighed, mocking her friend.

"What!" Eryn inquired instantly. Prodding her to reveal what her thoughts were.

"Nothing, I was just thinking about how skeptical you were when I first put you on to that pen pal site. Now you're all Ms. cuddlely love puppet letting your emotions pull you every which way and I don't have to tell you who the puppet master is," Jess said showing a bit of good natured envy.

"Girl bye," Eryn urged playfully. Not wanting to be reminded of her previous relationship with Avery, which nearly led to an emotional break down and Jess bringing her to the website Someone For Everyone dot com in the latter of it all.

***

See Eryn was raised an only child in the suburban area of Cherry Hill, New Jersey. The goddess-like marvel of bi-racial parents, to wit a Caucasian mother of which she inherited her fair porcelain skin, yellowish green eyes, and auburn hair. An African-American father whose side of the family she acquired her curvy physical attributes. Standing at a mere 5' 6", bearing a athletic build for the greater part of her life having been a softball fanatic, following in her mother's footsteps of sports in high school.

This subsequently earned her a four year scholarship at Temple University, at the tender age of seventeen. There she met Avery, who at first seemed charming but in time starting showing signs of his womanizing ways. After four to six months of dating the two decided to go steady.

With A being her first official boyfriend she became fairly attached to him, hence prompting her to tolerate his eventual cheating and manipulative ways, which became apparent approximately seven months after the relationship was officialized. After about a year into the relationship, Eryn allowed Avery to claim her innocence in an attempt to reshift the dynamic of control.

Which started out as a sweet, romantic, and compassionate union between them suddenly came to a halt just three years into the making.

Unsuccessfully trying to reconcile the now tarnished bond they once shared at his own misdeeds. One night during a big fraternity house party, Avery showed up at her off-campus housing door pissy drunk, after having had left the frat party early.

The same party Eryn declined her then roommate Jesenya's request to attend to stay back to study for an upcoming exam.

Eryn elegantly glides across the walkway from her bed to the door in a sheer night gown shirt. Not expecting anyone she readily responds to the exaggerated three taps on the door.

"Who is it?" she inquired.

"It's A," the voice responded from the other side of the door.

What the fuck is he doing here, she thought. "What do you want Avery, cause I really don't have time for this right now," she questioned with authority.

"I just want to talk shorty," he said using the name he affectionately called her.

"About what?" She urged, still standing on the other side of the door.

"Us," he simply replied.

"There is no us Avery, I keep trying to tell you that. You bartered US off for all the lies you've told and all the other women you had on the side," she said now becoming emotional.

"I know shorty and I'm sorry. Ain't none of them bitches mean shit to me, love. None of 'em could ever compare to what we built," A said, prying at her to open the door.

Eryn remained silent at that point contemplating the love she still had for Avery.

He then continued knowing that he was chipping away at her hardened facade. "I just want to see your face shorty. I've missed you love," A lastly retorted before hearing the dead-bolt latch snap back,

148

and the door, squeaking slightly open only to reveal the sliding security lock, preventing it from being any further ajar. The dim light from the room illuminated her beautiful face in the crack of the door, giving her skin a glowing complexion.

"You hurt me," she managed to say through a crackling voice.

"I know baby and I'm sorry," A persisted.

Now smelling the alcohol reeking from his breath, pores, and clothing trailing the words he spoke, Eryn angrily questioned his true motives for showing up at her door.

Avery too, becoming a bit agitated himself with the back and forth coy inquisitions; having history of not being able to hold his temper together very long. A firmly states, "Listen love, I just came here to talk. You won't return any of my phone calls and I'm really trying to see you. Open the door shorty, you know how I feel about having people in my business," he warned.

"No, Avery. You're already drunk please just leave," Eryn pleaded.

"What!" A interjected, feeling challenged by her rejection.

"Avery, please just leave," she continued.

"Fuck you got another nigga in there or some shit," A bitterly suggested.

"No Avery. Why are you acting so crazy?" Eryn asked being familiar with A's up-bringing, he having shared with her the intimate details of the abusive relationship his parents fostered. The binge drinking that caused his father to have occasional blackout spells, and how he was often isolated to his room while his father entertained his buddies.

Despite his financially secure living conditions, his father took every opportunity to admonish the family about his bread winning abilities. His mother too a victim; a frail woman succumbing to the same discourtesies, often afraid to come to her son's aide compelled Avery to suppress his emotions and become one with his solitude.

That childhood anger and resentment still brewing in his veins, Avery was surely to fall into the shoes of his father one way or the other.

The next action that followed was her trying to close the door in an attempt to put a more secured distance between them. A then used his foot as a door stop to prevent her from closing it. Now even more infuriated that she tried to close him out, caused him to go into an enraged state.

He allowed his drunken temperament to takeover, bestowing a storm of derogatory names. A then proceeds to hit the door with his shoulder once... twice... a third time and the door gave way as Eryn struggled to keep her attacker out. Knocking her to the floor, A entered the room and closed the door behind himself.

Now at an advantage, A stood staring down on Eryn as she looked on in horror while he decided his next move. Not wanting to lose the opportunity, A helps Eryn to her feet but only to make an attempt at seducing her. He sloppily kissed her on the outside of her lips while fiercely handling her tender parts.

Notwithstanding his advances, Eryn never reciprocated the favor. She held her mouth shut as A tried to force his stiff tongue between her tightly sealed lips. Giving in for a brief moment, Eryn bit his tongue, pushed him away and ran for the door. A charged right after her, grabbed her from behind; locking his fingers in her hair and slammed her back down to the floor. She was winded by the impact of the fall and became even more reluctant to fight back now knowing his strength.

A pushed her over onto her back from her side and fixed himself between her legs. After fumbling with his belt buckle for a second, A then unfastened the button on his jeans and unzipped them. Ignoring her pleas, he snatched her panties at the crotch area, tearing them at the seam. A forcefully jammed his manhood inside of her; and Eryn cringed in pain as he eagerly humped himself into a selfish orgasm.

Avery left her there on the floor where he raped her. Eryn's roommate Jesenya arrived soon thereafter to find her still laying there in agony and disoriented, in the fetal position. Her sheer nightie scantly covering the bottom half of her derriere. She was taken aback by the scenery at first, not believing her eyes but then rushed to Eryn's aide. The two having already established a relationship throughout the time they've spent as roommates, Jess finds taking care of her with ease.

Jesenya drew her a hot bath using bath salts and other feminine products, and helped her dress her rough scratches and bruised body afterwards. She even occasionally had to function as her comforting pillow in the coming days of the attack, as Eryn snuggled under her for further reassurance.

Eryn never reported the incident as a residual result of feeling embarrassed and ashamed, coupled with the insecure notion that it was partly her fault and that broadcasting the situation would only diminish her popularity, due to the nature of the event. So often Jesenya was Eryn's rock and the person she confided in, bringing the girls even closer over the years.

Both Eryn and Jesenya completed their four year scholarships and kept close contact after graduation. After experiencing the brutal rape back in college Eryn never allowed herself to be that vulnerable to another man or even let one get close enough to hurt her again. So often times she maintained the status of single, Eryn found it much more appeasing to just focus on her career but even that couldn't fill the emptiness she felt from not being touched by a man.

Being the good friend, Jess sets her up on a few blind dates, not being fond of her friend being lonely, but to no avail none of these men seemed to pique the interest of a young Eryn.

Finally, as a last resort Jesenya pointed Eryn in the direction of a website called someoneforeveryone.com, a pen pal registry dedicated to lonely prisoners. There she met Bashan whose profile indicated that it was recently listed.

Even more so, upon clicking on to his picture read that:

> I'm looking for a woman to build with and/make life more meaningful. It doesn't necessarily have to be on a relationship level; I'm also open to friendship, casual conversation and/or anything else of a beneficial nature.
>
> I'm from New Jersey and while incarcerated I've so far acquired my Diploma, and recently became a certified Level One Carpenter. I have other plans in the making as well, but at the moment my main goal is to be a fairly successful small business owner upon release.
>
> I have a great sense of humor. I'm into music, writing, pictures, and spending time with family. I'm a good listener, a go getta' and pretty much as chivalrous as they come... But I'ma leave that for you to decide. I'm only a stamp away.

After viewing a ton of other profiles; skimming through the ones centered on slick talk and those of the perverts, wasting no time nor giving any energy to the too emotional, too vague, or too demanding ones. All the while thinking to herself aloud, "Damn they really do got someone for everyone."

At that, Eryn decided that Bashan's was the more sensible, though still thumbing the idea on whether to write or not.

The following week at a luncheon between the two girls, Jess would ask Eryn about visiting the site only to receive an unenthusiastic remark in return.

"I did but I don't really know about corresponding with someone who is in prison girl, especially someone I don't even know."

"Eryn be honest with me, did you find someone that caught your eye?" Jess asked energetically.

"Does it matter Jesenya?" Eryn countered questioned.

"Yes, it does matter Eryn, and you know you can't hide shit from me 'cause you always start partially biting the right side of your bottom lip every time you attempt to, just like you're doing now."

"It's that obvious, huh?" Eryn asked, now forming a slight smile.

"It always is Eryn, but that's beside the point. My whole thing is

154

that you should at least give it a try."

Jesenya carried on further while Eryn sat listening attentively. "You restrict yourself from love for all the wrong reasons. I get it though; I just want you to be happy," Jess said providing clarity for her friend.

"You said that your apprehension to write was behind you not wanting to contact a stranger in prison. Now that does make sense, but in all actuality every person you meet out in the streets starts out as a stranger too. And who the hell knows what was made of their past or former lives. What I'm saying Eryn is that just because someone is in prison does not make them inhumane or the scum of the earth for that matter," Jesenya defended.

She paused for a moment to think back before mentioning her cousin Cid, who was currently serving a thirty year sentence for the retribution killing over a slain friend during a bad drug deal. But continued, "I'm sure some of them niggas do actually deserve to be in there but all in all, they're still people with feelings. Most of them are very compassionate, understanding and are still someone's son or brother and in most cases someone's father, but are fucking lonely just like your workaholic ass. So give it a shot girl, you never know who you'll meet or what will happen. Worst case scenario, you can even write from a P.O. box under a fictitious name until you become comfortable enough to reveal your true identity."

That was all that had to be said for Eryn to reconsider her reluctance and started her first letter to Bashan with 'Hi my name is Eryn...'

***

"It ain't even that serious Eryn." Jesenya stated before adding, "But I'ma let you go anyway. Call me when you're finished getting everything situated with Bashan. Mwwah."

"Alright girl, mwwah back," Eryn responded concluding the conversation.

76142747R00098

Made in the USA
San Bernardino, CA
09 May 2018